AFFAIRS OF THE MIND

AFFAIRS OF THE MIND:

The Salon in Europe and America
From the 18th to the 20th Century

Edited by Peter Quennell

New Republic Books
Washington, D.C.

Published in 1980 by

New Republic Books
1220 19th Street, N.W.
Washington, D.C. 20036

Library of Congress Cataloging in Publication Data

Affairs of the mind.

    1. Salons—Addresses, essays, lectures.
2. Europe—Intellectual life—Addresses, essays,
lectures.   3. United States—Intellectual life—
Addresses, essays, lectures. I. Quennell,
Peter, 1905-
GT129.A36   394   79-27612
ISBN 0-915220-57-1

Printed in the United States of America

ACKNOWLEDGEMENTS

The illustrations have been reproduced by kind permission of
the following:

Bilderdienst Süddeutscher Verlag, Munich, 1, 14; Ullstein
Bilderdienst, Berlin, 2, 29; Archiv für Kunst und Geschichte,
copyright Leihweise, 3; The Mansell Collection, 4, 5, 6, 10, 11,
12, 18, 33; The Wallace Collection, Crown copyright, 7; BBC
Hulton Picture Library, 9, 16, 17, 20, 26; Fitzwilliam Museum,
Cambridge, 13; *History Today*, 19; Grenfell Family Papers, 24,
25; National Portrait Gallery, Smithsonian Institution,
Washington, DC, 28; Paul Ybarra, 30; The Bettmann Archive,
32, 34; Sir Rupert Hart-Davis, 35; Sotheby's and Sir Cecil
Beaton, 36; Popperfoto, 37. All other photographs are from the
Weidenfeld & Nicolson archives.

Acknowledgement is made to Eyre Methuen, Ltd. for
permission to reprint *"Ich der Uberlebende"* (English translation by Bruce Cook). Copyright in the original: "Gedichte in
Exil" © copyright by Stefan S. Brecht, 1964. Copyright in the
translation © Stefan S. Brecht, 1980.

CONTENTS

AFFAIRS OF THE MIND

THE SALON

Peter Quennell

Between conversation and civilization, the art of talking and the art of living, there has always been a vital link. The most intelligent animals, modern zoologists tell us, from the whale and the dolphin to the gorilla and the chimpanzee, not only lead extremely sociable lives but engage in their own kind of talk; and every human culture, the historian would surely agree, has had a solid conversational basis and has depended on the lively exchange of ideas, and of the thoughts and feelings whence ideas spring. The ancient Greeks, for example, were passionate talkers; and so, indeed, were sixteenth-century Englishmen, whose love of talking while walking inspired the architects they employed to add a spacious long gallery to the Elizabethan "great house." Sir Walter Raleigh's "School of Night", a group of free-thinking poets and far-looking scientists that included Christopher Marlowe, Thomas Hariot and the "Wizard Earl" of Northumberland, was, no doubt, the earliest English salon; and Sir Philip Sidney's sister, Lady Pembroke, and Penelope Rich, sister to Shakespeare's friend and patron Lord Southampton, are said to have gathered around them brilliant assemblages of like-minded intellectuals.

ſ   It was in Paris, however, at the beginning of the seventeenth century, that the salon, as we understand the word today, first became a social influence. Catherine de Vivonne, Marquise de Rambouillet, had been married at the age of twelve to Henri IV's Grand Master of the Royal Wardrobe and obediently followed him

10

to Court; but the boisterousness of court life offended her sensitive nature; and she gradually withdrew. Then in 1618—the year of Raleigh's death—she inherited a Parisian town-house, the Hôtel de Pisani near the Louvre, and rebuilt it as the Hôtel de Rambouillet according to her personal design. For large and lofty apartments she substituted a series of *cabinets*, little rooms that suited small gatherings and quiet private conversations. Her own room was styled the *chambre bleue*—it was hung with blue velvet, trimmed with blue and silver—and there she received her guests, who, during her salon's heyday, included Corneille, the young Bossuet, La Rochefoucauld and Saint-Evremont, stretched on a comfortable *lit de repos* rather than seated on a straight-backed chair. Though fundamentally a serious woman—"all her passions are subject to reason", decided the famous novelist Mademoiselle de Scudéry— she had a "gay, light-hearted manner"; and she brought into the art of conversation a new reflective and imaginative tone. Critics objected that talk at the Hôtel de Rambouillet was inclined to be pretentious; and, toward the end of Catherine's reign, Molière, in his first popular triumph, *Les Précieuses Ridicules*, made sharp fun of such intellectual gatherings. But, by that time, her parties had lost their vogue; and Mademoiselle de Scudéry's far more 'precious' Saturday salons were rapidly replacing them.

Madame de Rambouillet died in 1665, Mademoiselle de Scudéry in 1701; and the eighteenth century, of course, was the salon's Golden Age, when Madame Geoffrin, Madame du Deffand and Mademoiselle de Lespinasse, among others far too numerous to mention, attracted admirers from all over Europe. Madame Geoffrin was perhaps the most appealing. Although she corresponded with crowned heads—Maria Theresa of Austria, Catherine the Great of Russia and King Stanislas of Poland—she was herself a worthy *bourgeoise*, married to a rich manufacturer who was seldom noticed at his wife's assemblies; and, although she enjoyed the company of learned men, she did not pretend to be an intellectual. Nor had she much use for advanced political notions, despite the fact that the revolutionary *encyclopédistes* constantly surrounded her. If a talker threatened to exceed the prescribed limit, with a phrase she often used—"*Voilà qui est bien!*"—she would quietly check his flow. But, since she recognised distinction and appreciated eloquence, her guests were always worth hearing; and a multitude of foreign Grand Tourists felt honoured to attend

PETER QUENNELL

her salon. Among her British visitors were David Hume, Edward Gibbon and the exiled "patriot" John Wilkes.

Eighteenth-century salons and the ladies who kept them, both English and French, form a large and highly complex theme; and in the present volume we have limited ourselves to the nineteenth and the first half of the twentieth century. Our heroines range from Juliette Récamier, who revived the Parisian salon during the Napoleonic epoch, to Emerald Cunard, whose drawing-room at the Dorchester Hotel remained a centre of life and gaiety and stimulating conversation throughout the darkest wartime years. As personalities, these two gifted women were remarkably dissimilar, Lady Cunard being impetuous and high-spirited and herself a ready conversationalist, while Madame Récamier was always gentle and demure and listened more often than she talked. But, as hostesses, they shared an important trait. Not only were they devoted to social life; but they were genuinely attached to their fellow men and women, and sought to elicit the most valuable and characteristic qualities of every newcomer they welcomed. While Madame Récamier's approach was subtly encouraging, Lady Cunard's method was to amuse and tease and, occasionally, provoke. The conversations she directed were never dull; and, should they introduce a touch of fantasy, which might rise at length to wild extravagance, nobody was better pleased. Forty years have passed since Lady Cunard's death; and I doubt if we shall see her like again. For the salon was the product of a leisured society; and the twentieth century allows us so little leisure that we have begun to forget the art of using it. How agreeably and profitably it was once used, by cultivated people who valued ideas, admired eloquence and delighted in one another's company, is the absorbing topic of the present book.

THE SALON

RAHEL VARNHAGEN
Tragic Muse of the Romantics

Hilde Spiel

When Rahel Varnhagen, in her fifty-fourth year, entered a Berlin assembly on the arm of her husband, a young actress named Karoline Bauer took a good look at the pair and, later, set down her impression with a candour unusual among her contemporaries. She portrayed the woman at whose feet sages, nobles, statesmen and poets had sat for more than three decades, as small, rather plump, with no waist at all, untidy brown locks over a beautiful brow, kind deep-blue eyes with long lashes, sharp Jewish features and a physiognomy that breathed goodwill and high intelligence. Karl August Varnhagen von Ense, on the other hand, "who created a servile cult of his wife, watched her, noted down everything she said and bore a triumphant smile on his indistinct, vain, bun-shaped face, quite obviously exulting in the pride of possessing such a famous wife."

It is the only unkind description handed down to us of this idol of her age and her devoted companion. Yet Rahel and her husband come alive far more vividly in Karoline Bauer's words than in the eulogies and flatteries that the Romantics used to shower upon one another. The eminence of that great hostess, philosopher, philanthropist and wit is by no means diminished, while the love and admiration her husband evidently felt for her helps to explain the ease, serenity and dignity with which Rahel, no beauty at any time, inspired friendship and affection even in her latter years.

A native of Berlin, like Fanny von Arnstein, she was born in 1771, the offspring of a Jewish family that enjoyed Royal protection. Her father, a diamond merchant, clever, witty and highly gifted, did not enjoy so important a position as Fanny's father Daniel Itzig. Marcus Levin adored his daughter, but he was a tyrannical parent. Proud of his eldest and cleverest child, he loved to see her shine in his house, which, since he was also a money-lender, many artists, actors and aristocrats frequented. He would not allow her, however, any personal freedom. Though she mourned for him, she must have felt some relief when he died in 1789. Soon afterwards, her mother, who appears to have been quarrelsome, selfish and mean, threw her out; and Rahel installed herself in an attic in Jägerstrasse 54.

The address is important; for here, during the same year, the first great salon of the dawning Romantic age was established. It was not the first salon in Berlin; the scholars and thinkers of the Prussian capital had been accustomed to meeting in Moses Mendelssohn's house and, later, in that of Doctor Marcus Herz. The physician's handsome wife, Henriette, reigned among his visitors, who paid homage both to her beauty and to her husband's wisdom and learning; and it was there that Rahel met the French revolutionary Mirabeau, the brothers Humboldt, the Counts Dohna and Bernstorff, the poet Friedrich von Schlegel and the Swedish diplomat von Brinkmann—all of whom, in due course, moved on to Rahel's garret in Jägerstrasse. Henriette, tall and swan-like, a statuesque figure swathed in melancholy, the "tragic muse of the Romantic writers," lacked the powers of reasoning, the penetrating insight, the quick flashes of humour and conversational gifts that Marcus Levin's small plump daughter could supply.

Three years earlier, this eighteen-year-old girl had begun to surround herself with a circle of ardent friends and admirers. Frederick the Great had now been succeeded by his nephew, Frederick William the Second; and the young king was not only a lecher and weakling, who revoked the tolerant laws of his uncle and re-introduced a limited form of censorship, but also surrounded the throne with an atmosphere of dissipation. The Berlin of his time, as described by the sculptor Schadow, was dedicated to every kind of luxury and self-indulgence; "the whole of Potsdam was like a brothel; all the families there wanted to be in touch with the king, and their wives and daughters were offered in competition. . . ." Meanwhile, noblemen who had been infected by the Enlightenment sought the company of intellectual Jews, whom they could emulate, and at whose houses they could flaunt their own knowledge.

HILDE SPIEL

In the mixed and unstable society of the last decade of the eighteenth century, and up to 1806, the Jewish salons, especially that of Rahel Levin, became the meeting-place of all outsiders of the upper and middle class—aristocrats, actors, emancipated women, writers and philosophers. In those years, Rahel received members of the Royal Family, like Prince Louis Ferdinand of Prussia and his sister, Princess Radziwill, noblemen like Count Tilly and Wilhelm von Burgstorff, famous actors like Fleck and Unzelmann, the great singer Madame Marchetti, picturesque characters such as the Bohemian Countess Pachta, who had deserted her husband for an untitled lover, and the Countess Schlabrendorf, who wore men's clothes and was expecting an illegitimate child, but, at the same time, important Romantic poets, like Friedrich Schlegel, the brothers Tieck, Brentano, Chamisso, Fouqué, Jean Paul and the great scholar Schleiermacher. From five in the afternoon until well into the night, "*tout Berlin*" assembled in Rahel's tiny garret; and to all she dispensed what she called her "attic truths".

Louis Ferdinand, son of the youngest brother of Frederick the Great, received her wise and sympathetic comments on the problems that he put to her, and used to call Rahel his "moral midwife, who delivers one so softly and painlessly that a gentle feeling comes to surround even the most tormenting ideas." His complicated love affairs, his political views, which clashed with those of his Royal cousin, and his ideological waverings were all treated by her with candour and understanding. Her acid remarks were reserved for others; her own friends were never touched by her biting wit. Later, after the end of the century, she made the acquaintance of Friedrich von Gentz, that iridescent figure who later became an Austrian statesman and a frequenter of Fanny von Arnstein's salon; and it was Gentz who paid her a high compliment: "Do you know, my dear," he asked, "why our relationship is so great and perfect? You are an endlessly productive and I am an endlessly receptive being. You are a great man; I am the first of all women who ever lived. That is, had I been a woman physically, I would have set my foot upon the globe."

Yet the fact that only an outsider, a "stopgap of society," as Rahel's biographer Hannah Arendt puts it, could play that particular part at that particular time never escaped her. Of all the great Jewish women of the Enlightenment and Romantic age, Rahel suffered most from her Jewishness. It is a recurrent theme in

RAHEL VARNHAGEN

everything she said about herself. During a fit of depression, she reviewed her life in later years as follows: "I was Jewish," she said, "not pretty, ignorant, without *grâce, sans talents et sans instruction*." And in her correspondence with a friend of her youth, David Veit, a Jewish student of medicine, she once complained:

> I have a fantasy that some extraterrestrial being, when I was pushed into this world, drove those words into me with a dagger: "Yes, have feeling; see the world as few others see it; be great and noble. Nor can I deprive you of an eternal way of thinking." One piece of advice, however, was forgotten: "Be a Jewess!" And now my life is one long bleeding to death. Keeping quiet may put it off; every movement to still it is a new death; and immobility is possible for me only in death . . . I can trace every ill, every misfortune, every misery to that.

The fame of her intelligence and social prowess soon spread throughout the various German kingdoms and dukedoms. Goethe, when he was at Karlsbad in the summer of 1795 and found himself staying near her, gladly received, and conversed with, Rahel. He recognized her "original" mind, never lost contact with her, and paid her a visit in 1815, when they both happened to be in Frankfurt. She retained her admiration for him all her life, and disliked the second school of Romantic writers as much for their unkind attitude towards Goethe as for their mystagogic leanings. In fact, while she moved with the *Zeitgeist* and considered herself a friend of Friedrich von Schlegel—whose *Lucinde* was the archetypal wild Romantic novel—she clung to the tenets of the late Enlightenment, to classicism and to the idealistic philosophy of Fichte, Schleiermacher and Humboldt. Though Gentz once told her, "You are Romanticism itself; you were that even before the word was invented," Rahel's clear-headed humanism remained the overriding force of her existence.

Romantic she seems to have been, at least in her earlier years, with regard to lovers and suitors. Often disappointed in men, she continued to fall in love, fiercely and with a fervour that in others she would have discouraged or even derided. Her first betrothal was to the fair and blue-eyed Count Karl von Finkenstein. The break, in 1799, left her desolate, but she bore him no grudge: "He was as innocent," she said of him, "as the axe that beheads a great man." Her "greatest turpitude" over, she met a Basque gentleman, the Secretary at the Spanish Embassy Don Raphael d'Urquijo, and again received a promise of marriage; but in 1804 the affair ended.

HILDE SPIEL

Another of the handsome young aristocrats whose affection she desired and won was Alexander von der Marwitz, later to lose his life in the Prussian War of Liberation. Though she denied she was a snob—"Noblemen I often love, the nobility never"—she wrote to Varnhagen on his receiving a title: "So long as there are noblemen, one must be ennobled too." Marwitz thought her the greatest woman on earth. Yet when the time came for her to settle down and choose a permanent companion she decided to marry Varnhagen.

In 1800, Rahel's brother Ludwig converted to Christianity and called himself Robert—a surname that for a while she herself adopted. While her first salon was in existence, however, and she was still accepted for what she was worth, the thought of altering her status never entered Rahel's mind. For another six years she remained the leader of intellectual society. In 1803, at the house of a factory-owner, she had made the casual acquaintance of Varnhagen, an ambitious young man fourteen years her junior. At the time, she took little notice of him. These were her great days when the future hero of Saalfeld, the "Prussian Alcibiades" and unhappy victim of his own patriotic fervour, Louis Ferdinand, as well as the elite of arts and letters, sat at her feet. A terrible awakening lay ahead. On October 27, 1808, Napoleon entered Berlin and swept away not only the Prussian Royal family, but the whole spiritual and social life of the city as it had existed since the days of Frederick the Great.

"What has become of the time," Rahel lamented in 1818, "when we were all together? It went under in 1806." The leisurely intimacy in which the elite had spent their time was replaced by hatred of the French occupying forces, clandestine plans to overthrow them, and a new patriotism that destroyed the former tolerant acceptance of outsiders. While Rahel's family fortunes dwindled, the whole structure of the Jewish salon collapsed. "Never again," writes Hannah Arendt, "was Rahel to stand in the centre of a representative circle without representing anything but herself." The salon, as she knew it, gave way to secret societies, or to unions such as Achim von Arnim's "Christian-German Table-Society", which excluded from membership "Women, Frenchmen, Philistines and Jews". Though the Jews now sided with the most fervent Prussians, a new anti-Semitism developed from the love for Prussia and hostility towards the free-thinking Napoleon.

In 1808, Rahel was obliged to leave Jägerstrasse and move to a cheaper apartment; but in that year, having lost many of her former circle, she again met Varnhagen, who courted her with an admiration that for some time she had missed. He announced that she was "a genuine person, a wonderful creation of God in its purest and most perfect type; everywhere nature and spirit in a fresh breath of change; everywhere organic form, vibrating fibre, sympathetic union with the whole of nature; everywhere original and naive utterings of mind and emotion, great in innocence and intellect . . . purest goodness, most beautiful and active charity, most subtle respect for any kind of personality." Two people destined to complement one another's character and mode of being had recognized their destiny at last. Soon after their second encounter, Rahel gave Varnhagen nearly three thousand letters that she had received from or written to important men and women; and these were to form the backbone of Varnhagen's posthumous publication of her correspondence.

Her relations with Varnhagen, nevertheless, were not steady, or marked by fidelity on either side, for a number of years. Varnhagen who, in 1809, saw active service in Austria, had struck up an affair with a pretty married woman, Fanny Hertz, and for a long time wavered between her and Rahel; Rahel had met von der Marwitz and felt torn between him and Varnhagen. It was in 1810, deprived of the general acclaim to which she had been accustomed, that Rahel adopted the name of Robert. Between that year and the defeat of Napoleon in 1813, she collected funds for the Prussian War of Liberation, helped to rouse patriotic feeling and nursed the wounded, so far as her feeble health and reduced circumstances would permit. But she knew only too well that her position as Berlin's foremost intellectual hostess, for the moment at least, could not be restored.

In the autumn of 1814 she decided to be baptized and to marry Varnhagen; a month later, she followed him to Vienna, where he was a member of the Prussian diplomatic mission at the Congress. All that winter and much of the next year she spent in Vienna, generally accepted as the Christian wife of Embassy Councillor Karl August Varnhagen von Ense. She was plagued by rheumatism and none too happy at the splendid receptions in Fanny von Arnstein's house, which she often visited. It was only when, in June 1815, Fanny moved to her country house at Baden near Vienna, and Varnhagen left her in the Arnstein's care, that Rahel began to appreciate their hospitality. At Baden, surrounded by "divine country," as she described it with Romantic passion, she enjoyed

HILDE SPIEL

social life on a slightly smaller scale. Fanny received the local worthies and some illustrious summer guests at tea parties; and Rahel, used to more select company, could again shine. Amid conservative visitors, she praised the French peasantry whom she deemed innocent of Napoleon's crimes and quickly won over her audience.

> Before they had all held different opinions. When I dared to say all this, they became their own opponents, with laughter and applause, and silence! But to dare such a thing one must judge the moment, see the brink at which, in spirit, those bored minds are standing, and must not be accused of personal interest, not even of disputatiousness. Oh, why am I no official personage! No Princess! (There you are right about me.) As true as God is alive! I had a good effect on them, that I can see. Also I am well-liked in the whole house.

Thus Rahel in a letter to her husband. She had regained her self-assurance, had found security in her marriage and once more prepared herself for a role in the world of high society and erudition. During the next few years, however, she was to remain the wife of a Prussian Chargé d'Affaires in the small residential capital of the German state of Baden, Karlsruhe, where Varnhagen had taken up this post. It was only on their return to Berlin in 1819 that she could renew former contacts and establish her second salon in Französische Strasse 20, with Varnhagen at her side.

This second salon, less brilliant perhaps but socially much more widely accepted, had a more political and scholarly aspect. Varnhagen brought his diplomatic friends and such academics as he knew; but it was his wife who remained the great attraction. Many years earlier, when Madame de Staël had come to Berlin, she had told Brinkmann, at whose house she met Rahel: "You did not exaggerate; she is astonishing! I can only repeat that Germany is a mine of genius, of which one knows neither the treasures nor the depth." Again, Rahel found recognition as a German genius, though her claim lay solely in her intelligence, her spontaneous wit and her ability to drive straight to the heart of every topic, as well as in the originality of her approach. Heinrich Heine, who stayed at her house in 1821, called her "the woman with the most *esprit* in the universe". Though there were times when they quarrelled, he was the only writer of the new generation close to her. In fact, so devoted was he to Rahel that he once said: "On my collar should be the words '*J'appartiens à Madame Varnhagen.*'" The great

Austrian dramatist Grillparzer, when, in 1829, he visited a sick and much-reduced Rahel, simply stated that never in his life had he had "a better and more interesting talk".

After her return to Berlin, Rahel began to ail and age even more visibly than she had done in middle life. Politically, the skies had darkened. Napoleon, to many a scourge, to others the most modern man in Europe, had made way for the powers of a narrow-minded and intolerant restoration. The wars had ended; but everywhere freedom of thought and the belief in the rights of man were curtailed. Anti-Semitism was rampant even among Achim von Arnim's friends, though he and especially his wife Bettina were fond of Rahel, and often attended her salon. There they encountered Hegel, the great historian Leopold von Ranke, both Humboldts and the aged Schleiermacher. If no Royal prince graced Rahel with his presence, she had found an exalted admirer in the person of Prince Hermann von Pückler-Muskau, creator of magnificent gardens, and was often invited to Muskau to see the results of his art.

In 1829 the Varnhagens moved to Mauerstrasse, and there set up their last salon. About this time, Rahel's chest trouble had become acute, and she had to look for airier surroundings. When two years later the cholera raged in Berlin, killing, among others, Hegel, she was laid up in bed though she herself had escaped the disease. She read much, mostly the works of Saint-Simon, of whom she had become an ardent follower. "I am the deepest Saint-Simoniste," she wrote a year before her death. "My whole belief is in the conviction of progress, of the perfectibility and development of the universe to even better understanding and welfare in the highest sense." Finally, this daughter of Enlightenment and friend of the Romantics took up mysticism and declared an interest in the French theosopher Louis-Claude de Saint-Martin, who became her greatest "révélateur", leading her "to experience God in contemplation"; but, she added, "he doesn't make me better than I am." Saint-Simon did; her real aim, like his, was "incessant improvement of the moral, intellectual and physical existence of the most numerous and poorest classes". Infected by his ideas, Rahel finally turned into a utopian socialist.

During the summer and autumn of 1832, the year of Goethe's death, Rahel was still visited. In March 1833, her ceaselessly active mind, lodged in an increasingly fragile body, was, at length, extinguished. Varnhagen, who had created a cult around her even when she was alive, now began to turn her into a legend. His

HILDE SPIEL

memoirs, his diaries, his publication of many volumes of Rahel's correspondence made posterity aware of what so far only the wide circle of her friends had known—that there had lived a woman who (to reverse the words of Gentz) had she been born a man, would have set her foot upon the globe.

LADY BLESSINGTON

A Literary Club for Editors

Prudence Hannay

During the first half of the nineteenth century two London hostesses, Lady Holland and Lady Blessington, entertained the most intellectual society of the day; the fact that their visitors were almost exclusively male was due to a similar misfortune: both had contravened the established moral code. Irregularities in marriage were tolerated among the *haut ton* so long as the parties maintained an outward appearance of conformity; but neither Lady Holland nor Lady Blessington had obeyed the rules, and both were deemed ineligible to receive visits from ladies in the vanguard of society. In the case of Lady Holland, her critics at least knew what they blamed: her first marriage had been dissolved by Act of Parliament on the grounds of her liaison with Lord Holland. Lady Blessington's misfortune was that her contemporaries were unsure of what they were disapproving; her life was therefore plagued by rumours. Both ladies nevertheless accepted their fate and triumphed in their own sphere.

There were certain other similarities in their early lives, apart from unhappy marriages to men of unstable disposition. Each possessed great personal beauty and lively intelligence; and each had sought consolation in the world of books; so that later, when fortune smiled on them and they found themselves presiding over the best-known salons in London, they were able to attract intellectual guests. But the similarity ends; their temperaments were entirely different.

When Lady Blessington first opened her salon in 1831, she had been twice widowed; and she never remarried. At Seamore Place, off Park Lane, and later at Gore House in Kensington, she was herself the magnet. Her personal beauty, together with her gift of understanding, created a happily relaxed atmosphere in which her natural kindliness and charm broke down every barrier. As a conversationalist, she was full of fun and gaiety, a *raconteuse* who made even commonplace subjects fascinating. "She had a singular power"[wrote the literary critic Henry Chorley]"of entertaining herself by her own stories; the keenness of an Irishwoman in relishing fun and repartee, strange turns of language, bright touches of character . . . With eyes as quick as lightning, her resources were many and original."

On her debut at Seamore Place, she took her chosen society by storm. Joseph Jekyll, *littérateur*, wit and antiquary, described an evening there in the early days:

> George Colman, James Smith, Samuel Rogers and Thomas Campbell dined with me yesterday at a Parisian repast of much refinement given us by the Countess of Blessington. There was wit, fun, epigram and raillery enough to supply fifty county members for a twelvemonth. Miladi has doffed her widow's weeds and was almost in pristine beauty.

Of the guests whom Jekyll listed, Colman was Licenser and Examiner of Plays; James Smith co-authored with his brother the famous "Rejected Addresses", performed at the re-opening of the Drury Lane Theatre in 1812; Samuel Rogers, the banker-poet, was famous for his literary breakfasts; and Thomas Campbell, the Scottish poet, edited until 1830 *The New Monthly Magazine*.

Lady Blessington, christened Margaret Power in 1789, was the daughter of a handsome but irascible local official. A resident of County Tipperary, her father, finding himself in 1804 financially embarrassed, married off for a financial consideration his fifteen-year-old girl to an English Army officer, Captain Maurice St. Leger Farmer. It took her very little time to discover that Captain Farmer was sadistic and often violent. Life with him was so unendurable that she risked her father's fury by returning home after the first few months of marriage; and she never set eyes on her husband again. The experience killed her sexual feelings; the result was that she later channelled her naturally strong emotions into the motherly or

PRUDENCE HANNAY

sisterly role that she preferred. Her kindness became almost legendary. After her death one of her regular guests wrote:

> Hers was a life-diffusing happiness. Her kindness was instinct, yet ardent, as if it had been a passion, and above all women of her time she fascinated, and fascination is a moral grace for it has its source in the soul . . .

Shortly after she returned home, another Army officer had entered Margaret's life, this time with more agreeable results. Captain Thomas Jenkins, a man of means as well as of sympathy, appreciated her unhappy circumstances besides being deeply attracted by her beauty, and he therefore suggested that she accompany him to his estate in Hampshire. The suggestion was one she was particularly glad to accept, since she had heard that Captain Farmer was due home from foreign service and intended to reclaim his wife.

For ten years she lived under Jenkins's protection, with his mother and his sisters. That he was both warm-hearted and considerate is obvious; for it was during these peaceful years that she developed her keen interest in literature and the arts. Her protector was himself a man of culture, and she accompanied him on at least two visits to Paris. Little occurred to disturb the even tenor of her life until 1816, when Jenkins's friend, the affluent Irish peer Lord Blessington, visited them. Jenkins and Lord Blessington had much in common, apart from their genial temperaments and volatile dilettantism. Lord Blessington, recently widowed, fell in love with Margaret and offered her his hand in marriage. Thus it came about that Margaret Farmer was established in Manchester Square, while Lord Blessington occupied separate London apartments and patiently awaited the divorce action that he had filed on her behalf. This, however, proved unnecessary; for, early in 1818, news arrived of Captain Farmer's death following a drunken brawl. On February 16, Margaret became the Countess of Blessington at St. Mary's Church, Bryanston Square. Her husband was then thirty-four; she was twenty-seven.

Given the choice, Lord Blessington would have spent part of each year on his Dublin estate. In theory he disapproved of absentee landlords; in practice, however, he was a compulsive spendthrift, happy to settle in London and to travel abroad at his wife's command. During their first two years of marriage, they lived at 10 St. James's Square, where Lady Blessington gained her first experience as a London hostess. It came as no disappointment to learn that she would not be visited there by fashionable ladies, for her husband's genial temper and her own beauty and intelligence seemed to attract illustrious company. Regular guests in the political field included Castlereagh, Canning and Palmerston, as well as the Duke of Wellington and his brother Lord Wellesley; among artists David Wilkie, John Varley and Sir Thomas Lawrence, who was commissioned to paint the well-known portrait of his hostess that now hangs in the Wallace Collection. Among literary figures she welcomed Samuel Rogers, Thomas Moore, Joseph Jekyll and the elderly classical scholar, Dr. Samuel Parr, who referred to Lady Blessington as "most gorgeous", and rightly predicted that, "with her shrewd and masculine mind, she would be even more impressive in middle age than while in the lovely splendour of her youth."

It was in 1821 that Count Alfred d'Orsay first visited St. James's Square with his sister and brother-in-law, the Duc and Duchesse de Guiche. D'Orsay, an attractive, clever and charming twenty-year-old, quickly took Lord Blessington's fancy. The only son of the Bonapartist General d'Orsay, Alfred d'Orsay had managed to obtain a commission in the Bourbon Garde Royale, but he longed to emulate his gregarious sister's social life. When Lord Blessington invited him to accompany them on an extensive Continental tour, he seized the opportunity of resigning his commission; as it turned out, the trio was only parted by death. He shared the Blessingtons' interest in the decorative arts and in collecting precious bibelots; his hostess, being childless herself, came to regard him with the affection of a mother for a somewhat spoiled child. In August 1822 the party set out for the Continent, where they were to remain for the next eight years; when Lady Blessington finally returned to London, she came as a widow, for her husband had died of a stroke in Paris. It was generally believed that, despite his wife's restraining influence, he had spent rather too much of his fortune on wine.

During their years abroad, the Blessingtons had established many valuable friendships, especially with Lord Byron in 1823, and with Walter Savage Landor in 1827. Byron, on first meeting Lady Blessington in Genoa, described her as "very literary—and very pretty, even of a morning". For six weeks they met daily; and news of his death at Missolonghi within the year greatly saddened both

PRUDENCE HANNAY

the Blessingtons. They met Landor in Florence, and thus began one of Lady Blessington's deepest and most lasting friendships. Landor was in his early fifties and his recently-published *Imaginary Conversations* she already knew well. The association with a charming, intelligent and sympathetic woman was of enduring comfort to the able, crotchety, radical-minded writer. It set the seal on Lady Blessington's preference for literary society and, as time passed, many celebrated literary figures came to her salon through his introduction.

The terms of Lord Blessington's will had been somewhat curious. To his beloved wife he left a jointure of £2000 a year, the dwindling lease of his London house and some chattels—little enough for the life of elegant luxury to which she had become accustomed—while the bulk of his vast estate was bequeathed to Count d'Orsay, who in 1827 had married Lady Harriet Gardiner, Lord Blessington's fifteen-year-old daughter. Undoubtedly Blessington was a man of surprising and at times unfortunate whims; and, having lost his beloved only son, a boy of ten, in 1823, he had thereafter focused his paternal affection on d'Orsay, deciding that he should marry Harriet, although the pair were almost strangers. Lady Blessington inevitably drew severe censure upon herself by condoning this arrangement, even though, wishing to spare her step-daughter a repetition of her own experience, she had stipulated that the marriage should not be consumated for four years. Nevertheless, to many outside her own circle, the arrangement appeared to be a mask for her own liaison with d'Orsay. The fact that the d'Orsays spent their short married life under her roof did nothing to excuse her since, even after the marriage had broken up, d'Orsay was still her most constant visitor. But Lady Blessington herself, having no desire for such an attachment, seems to have been largely impervious to the suspicions she aroused. D'Orsay, moreover, had never been an *homme-à-femmes*. Although he was always popular with men his narcissism effectually eliminated any amorous interest in either sex.

Lady Blessington's first task, on resuming her London life, was to dispose of the lease of 10 St. James's Square; in its place she chose a house in Seamore Place, just south of Curzon Street. A young American poet, Nathaniel Parker Willis, has left a vivid word-picture of Lady Blessington and her new background. When he visited Seamore Place, with an introduction from Landor, soon after she had settled there in 1831, Willis was shown into a library lined with book-cases and mirrors, which had a deep window looking on to Hyde Park:

> The picture to my eye as the door opened was a very lovely one: a woman of remarkable beauty half buried in a *fauteuil* of yellow satin reading by a magnificent lamp suspended from the centre of an arched ceiling; sofas, couches, ottomans and busts arranged in rather a crowded sumptuousness through the room; enamel tables covered with expensive trifles in every corner . . .

They enjoyed a long conversation, chiefly about America; and, for the benefit of his American news column, Willis wrote:

> Lady Blessington is now (she confessed it very frankly) forty, her person is full but preserves all the fineness of an admirable shape and her complexion (an unusually fair skin with very dark hair and eyebrows) is of even a girlish delicacy and freshness. Her dress of blue satin was cut low and folded across her bosom in a way to show to advantage the round and sculpture-like curve and whiteness of a pair of exquisite shoulders . . . Her features are regular and expressive of the most unsuspicious good-nature. Add to all this a voice merry and sad by turns, yet always musical, and manners of the most unpretending elegance, yet even more remarkable for their winning kindness, and you have the prominent traits of one of the most lovely and fascinating women I have ever seen.

Willis gladly accepted an invitation for the following evening; and, this time, Lady Blessington received him in her drawing-room, which was even more elegant than the library. On walls covered in crimson damask hung numerous miniatures and gold-framed looking-glasses; the curtains, carpet and upholstery were also of crimson, fringed with gold. Lady Blessington, in full evening dress, "had six or seven gentlemen about her", among whom were Albany Fonblanque, editor of the *Examiner*; James Smith; Henry Bulwer, as distinguished in the diplomatic world as was his brother Edward in the literary milieu; the Duc de Richelieu; a German prince; a traveller from the Near East; and "the splendid person of Count d'Orsay." Conversation covered a variety of subjects, ranging from O'Connell's latest speech to the respective merits of Fenimore Cooper and Washington Irving. Towards midnight "Mr. Lytton Bulwer was announced. The author of *Pelham* ran up to Lady Blessington with the joyous heartiness of a boy let out of school."

PRUDENCE HANNAY

Edward Bulwer's introduction to Lady Blessington had occurred soon after she moved to Seamore Place. They were originally brought together by her need of money, for on her present income it was growing increasingly difficult to conduct a salon in her own style. But, some years earlier, Longmans had published a volume of her *Sketches of London Life*, and to write a further series seemed an obvious solution. Accordingly, she applied to *The New Monthly*, a journal owned by Charles Heath and edited by Edward Bulwer. Though in 1832, when they first met, he was only twenty-seven, Bulwer had already published five novels which she had read and much admired. "They amuse me less, but they make me think more," she had once remarked.

Her offer resulted in an agreement with the sub-Editor of the *New Monthly*, Samuel Carter Hall; she was to record, in a series of articles, her conversations with Lord Byron. Like many others, Hall succumbed to her charm at their first interview:

> A peculiarly Irish face, round, soft and smiling, a low musical voice with the occasional trace of a Dublin accent; she was perfectly unaffected and with no trace of self-distrust; indeed, she seemed conscious of power but with no ambition to exploit it.

The meeting had been soon followed by a visit from Bulwer himself; and, as had happened with Landor, this brilliant but difficult and basically lonely man found in Lady Blessington a deeply sympathetic, lifelong friend. Moreover, he brought in his wake his brother Henry and both the Disraelis, Isaac and Benjamin. By 1833 Seamore Place had become a favourite resort for literary society; and some preferred Lady Blessington's parties to the more formal evenings at Holland House. The doors of the salon were open from eight to twelve every evening; and a superb dinner was followed by some hours of conversation.

Many factors contributed to her success with men of letters. As a budding author herself, she came to be regarded as one of their fraternity. Her first novel, *The Repealers*, was published in 1833; and the popularity of her Byron series led Heath to offer her the editorship of *The Book of Beauty*, a newcomer to a very popular form of publication, the annual. The English literary scene at this time was particularly brilliant; while the reading public devoured the novels of Edward Bulwer, Jane Austen, Maria Edgeworth, Captain Marryat and the young Disraeli, topical sketches and other forms of journalism were thrown off by the rising generation of future novelists, such as Dickens, Thackeray and Harrison Ainsworth. The Blessington salon was accepted almost as a literary club for editors, journalists and publishers. Among the editors were Albany Fonblanque of the *Examiner*; William Jordan of the *Literary Gazette*, whose criticisms could make or mar a book; and Captain Marryat, owner-editor of the *Metropolitan Magazine*. But the staffs of many other journals—*The London, Fraser's, The Athenaeum, Blackwood's, The Gentleman's Magazine, Bently's Miscellany, New Monthly*, even the Tory *Quarterly* and the Whig *Edinburgh Review*—were also represented in her drawing-room. With her gift for discerning the man behind the mask, Lady Blessington, writing to Bulwer, thus described Fonblanque, a man of the most unprepossessing appearance, made worse by his untidy habits:

> Lay this man to your heart; he is one of those extraordinary men too good for the age in which they are born, too clever not to be feared instead of loved, and too sensitive and affectionate not to be grieved that it is so.

Several of these distinguished personages contributed to their hostess's *Book of Beauty*, if only as a mark of affection and respect—for example, the poet, Barry Cornwall; Henry Luttrell, whose conversation Lady Blessington likened to a "limpid stream" that "flows smoothly and brightly along, revealing the depths beneath its current"; Theodore Hook, a prolific journalist; and the artists, Landseer, Maclise and Sir Martin Archer Shee, President of the Royal Academy. Any of them might be found, evening after evening, at Seamore Place and, later, at Gore House. Dramatists, too, attended regularly, for playwriting was a fashionable occupation among literary men, whose work was often staged by William Macready, the actor-manager, at Covent Garden. Macready was another close friend of Lady Blessington's, though he complained that her dinners were too rich; and with him came Sir Thomas Noon Talfourd, usually known as "Serjeant Talfourd", a man of great eminence and charm, whose play *Ion* was produced by Macready with notable success. Talfourd was, in turn, a Member of Parliament, a leading member of the Bar, where he became Serjeant-at-Law, a Judge of the Court of Common Pleas, and a playwright and literary critic; and it was he who introduced the young Charles Dickens both to Lady Blessington and to Lady

PRUDENCE HANNAY

Holland. A number of eminent politicians were also regular visitors—Lords Durham, Brougham, Lyndhurst, Abinger and the Speaker of the House, Charles Manners Sutton, who had married Lady Blessington's sister Ellen. Whenever he visited England, Landor was often to be found at Seamore Place or Gore House, and sometimes stayed with his hostess for weeks at a time.

By 1836 Lady Blessington had begun to feel the need of a more countrified residence—still ostracized by her own sex, she dreaded walking out from Seamore Place—with a garden large enough for daily exercise, in peaceful surroundings, where she could write at ease. Thus, that spring, she moved to Kensington. Gore House, built in 1750, had once been the home of William Wilberforce, and stood amid three acres of gardens near the site of the present Albert Hall, a plain, three-storeyed building set back from the road behind a wall, with entrance gates at either end. The garden, with its lawns, flowerbeds, trees, pathways and even a pond, ran southwards towards Brompton Road.

Inside, drawing room, dining room and library were, as before, the main reception rooms; and Lady Blessington changed the colour-scheme of the library to apple-green, with white painted bookshelves divided by mirrors. Originally two rooms, it had supporting columns half across the centre, and ran the length of the house from north to south. There were two fireplaces. Lady Blessington's great armchair overlooked the garden at the far end.

From the moment Gore House opened its doors, her salon became more crowded than ever. "Where else," wrote Landor after his first visit, "can I find so much wit, so much wisdom; or, as the rest of the world may pretend, can it collect (but I doubt it) so much beauty?" When Charles Dickens arrived, still in his late twenties, he described his hostess as "wearing brilliantly—she has the gloss upon her yet," and compared Landor to "forty lions concentrated into one Poet."

By 1840 Lady Blessington had reigned almost supreme for nearly a decade. Her only serious rival was Lady Holland; but the two hostesses never met; nor had they any wish to do so. But Gore House and Holland House were equally distinguished, both from an intellectual and from a social point of view: one would think [wrote William Archer Shee, brother of Sir Martin]

> that such varied ingredients would not amalgamate well, but would counteract or neutralise each other, rather than form a mixture to the

LADY BLESSINGTON

taste of all, but such is not the case. Under the judicious and graceful presidency of the attractive hostess, the society that meets in her salon has a charm that few reunions of the most learned or the most witty can offer. She has the peculiar and most unusual talent of keeping the conversation in a numerous circle general, and of preventing her guests from dividing into little selfish *pelotons*. With a tact unsurpassed she contrives to draw out even the most modest tyro from his shell of reserve, and by taking an interest in his opinion gives him the courage to express it. All her visitors seem by some hidden influence to find their level, and they leave her house satisfied with themselves . . .

As the decade progressed, however, Lady Blessington appeared to have lost something of her old gaiety, the result, no doubt, of journalistic overwork and her grave financial problems. She was now supporting several members of her family and d'Orsay, too, with his insatiable extravagance. He, the great dandy, was a strain on her nervous system as well as on her purse. "It seems to me," wrote Bulwer to Fonblanque at this period, "as if d'Orsay's *blague* were too much for her; people who live with those too high-spirited always get the life sucked out of them." Meanwhile, Lady Blessington, still hard at work, was editing yet another annual, at Charles Heath's invitation. Delighted with the success of *The Book of Beauty*, he also commissioned her to edit *The Keepsake*. To Bulwer she had recently confided that "there are so few before whom one would condescend to appear otherwise than happy"; to which he had replied, "Bright heroism of a woman! It echoes all my wish but exceeds all my power."

Nevertheless, during those years, newcomers still thronged the salon: Dickens; John Forster, the youthful literary and dramatic critic of *The Examiner*; Richard Monckton-Milnes; and Thackeray, who all repaid their hostess's kindness with contributions to her annuals. Another regular visitor was Louis Napoleon Bonaparte, whose mother, ex-Queen Hortense of Holland, Lady Blessington had met in Rome many years earlier. Exiled at different times in America, Switzerland and England, the Pretender to the throne of France was not considered very prepossessing by his fellow guests at Gore House. "Short, thick and vulgar", wrote the diarist Charles Greville. Landor commented: "They say he is no fool—he looks like one, which is unusual in that family."

Towards the end of the decade, the end of Lady Blessington's career was almost in sight. D'Orsay, who had moved into Gore

PRUDENCE HANNAY

House, was liable to be arrested on behalf of his creditors if he emerged during daylight hours; and, early in 1849, Lady Blessington herself received an execution of debt from her dressmakers, whose bill, she knew, she could not meet. Accordingly, she put the entire contents of Gore House up for sale by auction. D'Orsay fled to the Continent, and she joined him in Paris that April. She would soon have learned that the proceeds of the sale enabled her to discharge all her debts, and d'Orsay's too, but early in June she suffered a seizure and died within a few hours. Epitaphs were composed both by Barry Cornwall and by Landor, who wrote in his tribute: "The benefits she conferred she could conceal but not her talents. Her own genius she cultivated with zeal, in others she encouraged its growth with equal assiduity."

LADY BLESSINGTON

LADY HOLLAND

An Elite English Circle

Prudence Hannay

A social elite [writes Lord David Cecil] has seldom been also a cultural
elite; certainly not in England. As Henry James pointed out, there was
often a distressing contrast between the stately and exquisite beauty
of England's great country houses and the dull philistine persons who
were their owners. But there have been exceptions, and a notable one
was Holland House in the early nineteenth century. . . where evening
after evening some of the most interesting and agreeable people in
England used to meet to discuss and discourse, to dine and to shine.
The company was predominantly male, for Lady Holland was a
divorced woman. . .

Born in 1771, Lady Holland was the only child of rich parents; her
father, Richard Vassall, owned large estates in Jamaica. But,
although she was an heiress, she received a somewhat casual
education, and found her best-loved companions on the
bookshelves of her father's well-stocked library in Golden Square,
where, as she wrote, "I was left entirely to follow my own bent." It
was a lonely existence; and the loneliness continued beyond
childhood; for, in 1786, her mother accepted on her behalf the
proposal of a forty-nine-year-old baronet, Sir Godfrey Webster,
Member of Parliament for Seaford. His bride, then barely sixteen,
possessed unusual beauty, unusual intelligence and, in due time,
great wealth. Sir Godfrey, however, who owned the Battle Abbey
Estate and lived at the Dower House, proved to be the worst
possible husband Mrs. Vassall could have chosen. Of meagre
intelligence, concerned only with country life, he grew more and

more exasperated by his wife's unwillingness to take any pleasure in his favourite pursuits. Between 1789 and 1794, she bore him three children; apart from this bond the couple had nothing in common; and Sir Godfrey became liable to bouts of violence. Elizabeth again sought consolation in reading—a further irritant to her bucolic husband.

In 1791, she persuaded Sir Godfrey to take her abroad. Their travels lasted five years; she never returned to the Abbey. The tour was a turning-point in her life. There were then many English travellers on the Continent; and the reports of Lady Webster's beauty and intelligence spread quickly. The Webster's route led them through France and Switzerland to Italy, where their second son was born. Finally, early in 1794, Elizabeth settled at Florence, while Sir Godfrey returned home on parliamentary business.

In his welcome absence, Lady Webster found herself entertaining, among other English visitors, Lord Granville Leveson-Gower and Henry Richard, third Lord Holland, two youthful aristocrats on the Grand Tour. Lord Granville was the handsomer; Lord Holland, though slightly lame, the livelier; and their hostess was in the mood for gaiety. "Lord Holland quite delightful", she wrote in her journal; "His gaiety beyond anything I ever knew, full of good stories. He seems bent upon politics." Indeed, this young peer, who had succeeded to the title as a baby, inherited in full measure the charm, intelligence and warmth of heart of his uncle Charles James Fox, who had played a large part in his upbringing.

Small wonder then that Elizabeth Webster succumbed to the delight of his daily companionship, or that he fell victim to her exceptional beauty. Before long the two were deeply in love; and, when Sir Godfrey returned to England for good in 1795, the liaison flourished. It was to remain a union of the utmost devotion for over forty years. Early in 1796, Elizabeth found herself with child by Lord Holland, and together they regained London; whereupon Sir Godfrey instituted divorce proceedings by Act of Parliament. The marriage was dissolved in July 1797; the lovers' wedding took place quietly two days later. Shortly afterwards, they moved into Holland House with their son, Charles Richard Fox.

Since Lord Holland's youth, Holland House had been in the hands of tenants; but he had always felt strongly attached to his ancestral home, the Elizabethan red-brick-and-stone house with its Dutch gables and various happy additions of the Stuart period, that stood just outside London in an extensive park that stretched from

PRUDENCE HANNAY

the present-day Holland Park Avenue to Kensington Road. Within its grounds were cottages, stables and farm buildings, besides Little Holland House, where Lord Holland's much-loved only sister Caroline and their youthful aunt Lady Elizabeth Vernon were soon to settle down for life.

Although she was now the *châtelaine* of a house she loved, Lady Holland immediately understood that she was likely to be ostracized by the Court, the Tory Party and London hostesses of the first rank. But with the Whig Party it was different; Lord Holland was a promising young politician; and Holland House soon became a natural meeting place of the Whigs—a role it would continue to fulfill until its owners' death. Even in those early days, politicians thronged to the Holland House salon: Sheridan, Tierney, Romilly, Whitbread, Charles Grey, William Lamb, Henry Brougham and George Canning, who shared with his host a profoundly classical scholarship and a hatred of the Slave Trade. The regular company also included literary men: Sir Philip Francis, "Monk" Lewis, Henry Luttrell, Samuel Rogers, besides Dr. Parr, himself a great classical scholar, and Joseph Jekyll.

From May 1799 onwards Lady Holland began to keep her famous "Dinner Books," a faithful record of each evening's visitors, who numbered as many as fifty. But excess of company never bothered her; indeed, she regarded an overcrowded table as an asset; and when, at a different period, Charles Greville spoke of "a true Holland House dinner," he was referring to the fact that there were two visitors too many, and that "Lady Holland had the pleasure of a couple of general squeezes, and of seeing her guests' arms properly pinioned." Samuel Rogers, indeed, believed this close-packing was one of the secrets of Lady Holland's social success; for "it added," she said, "to the conversableness and agreeableness."

Not until about 1810, however, did Holland House gain its unrivalled reputation as a salon. Lord and Lady Holland had spent some part of their early married life in foreign travel while their home was extensively restored; and during these years three children were born to them—Henry Edward Fox, the heir, and his sisters Mary and Georgiana. Travel had done much to restore Lady Holland's *amour propre*. Whereas at home she was often slighted, abroad she enjoyed a privileged status and received innumerable flattering invitations. Thus, during the Peace of Amiens, presentation to the First Consul and his wife in Paris was followed by an open invitation to evening assemblies at St. Cloud, a compliment that no doubt inspired Lady Holland's life-long affection for the Emperor. Many of the distinguished friends the Hollands had made abroad—for example, John Hookham Frere, the British Envoy to Spain, and his brother Bartle—afterwards regularly visited them at Kensington; and Dr. John Allen, scholar and physician, who had joined them on their travels, soon became, as family friend and librarian, a permanent member of their household. He held an important post. Lord Holland, a keen bibliophile, was continually increasing his collection; in the Long Library at Holland House much of their entertaining took place.

For a description of these evenings we must turn to Macaulay, who, years later, described the library to his sister:

> That venerable chamber, in which all the antique gravity of a college library was so singularly blended with all that female grace and wit could devise to embellish a drawing room. . . a long room with little cabinets for study branching out of it, warmly and snugly fitted up. The collection of books contains almost everything that one ever wished to read.
>
> A most excellent dinner was served in a fine long room, the wainscot of which is rich with gilded coronets, roses and portcullises—the Gilt Room. There are also a considerable number of very large and very comfortable rooms—the Yellow and Green Drawing Rooms, and the White Parlour— rich in antique carving and gilding, but carpeted and furnished with all the skill of the best modern upholsterers.

Visitors usually assembled in the Green Drawing Room (later named Sir Joshua's Room), on the first floor to the north side of the house, then moved to the Gilt Room for dinner, and next passed through the Yellow Drawing Room to the Long Library, which ran full length from north to south, where coffee was served and the remainder of the evening was spent.

Lord Holland had implicit faith in his wife's judgment, both in the arrangement of the house and in the choice of guests. There was one marked difference between Lady Holland's salon and that of her rival hostess, Lady Blessington—no one ever entered Holland House without a formal invitation. But Lord Holland possessed an extraordinary gift for friendship. Conversation was one of his chief delights; he showed a rare combination of tolerance, wit, mimicry and anecdote, together with the ability to put the most bashful newcomer entirely at ease. When he limped to his place at the

PRUDENCE HANNAY

dining table, he seldom knew just who his guests might be; but he could feel sure that they formed as stimulating a company as he could have possibly desired.

Both Lady Holland and Lady Blessington were themselves gifted conversationalists; but the talk at Holland House tended to be directed by the hostess; and she cut short, with a tap of her fan, any conversations that did not please or any habits that offended her. Dreading boredom, nervous and highly strung, she had never quite overcome the basic unhappiness of her earlier life, even now that she lived in the radius of Lord Holland's sunny nature. He "always came down to breakfast," Samuel Rogers recorded, "like a man upon whom some good fortune has suddenly fallen." Volatile and imperious, once she enjoyed the newfound freedom of her second marriage, Lady Holland had determined to grasp and hold fast the reins in all future relationships. Her husband's devotion and tolerance tended merely to accentuate her domineering traits. As Macaulay wrote after their first meeting:

> She is certainly a woman of considerable talents and great literary acquirements. To me she was excessively gracious; yet there is a haughtiness in her courtesy which, even after all that I had heard of her, surprised me. The centurion did not keep his soldiers in better order than she keeps her guests. It is to one "Go" and he goeth; and to another "Do this" and it is done. "Ring the bell, Mr. Macaulay." "Lay down that screen, Lord Russell, you will spoil it." "Mr. Allen, take a candle and show Mr. Cradock the picture of Bonaparte." Lord Holland, is on the other hand, all kindness, simplicity and vivacity.

Yet there was another side to her character. *Au fond*, she possessed an unsuspected sensitivity. Her guests tolerated her dictatorial manners, secure in the knowledge that beneath them lay a genuine warmth and generosity of heart. Thus she aroused deep affection, even though her strictures might cause temporary resentment. She so offended Charles Greville and Lord Durham that they gave up visiting her salon for some years; "and then we met again," wrote Greville, "as if there had been no interruption, and as if we had been living together constantly." Nevertheless, as her favourite physician put it:

> There was in reality *intention* in all she did; and this intention was the maintenance of power which she gained and strenuously used, though not without discretion, in fixing its limits. No one knew better when to

LADY HOLLAND

change her mood and to soothe by kind and flattering words the
provocation she had just given and was very apt to give. . . and here
she was aided by a native generosity of mind which never failed to
show itself in kindness where kindness was wanted.

Until his departure from England in 1816, Byron was a frequent
visitor at Holland House; in his *Journal* he wrote of one occasion,
when the fame of the salon was gathering momentum:

> Sunday I dined with Lord Holland; large party—among them Sir S.
> Romilly and Lady Ry—General Sir Somebody Bentham, a man of
> science and talent. . . Horner, *the* Horner, an Edinburgh Reviewer, an
> excellent speaker in the "Honourable House"; Lord John Russell and
> others, "good men and true." Holland's society is very good; you
> always see someone or other in it worth knowing. Stuffed myself with
> sturgeon, and exceeded in champagne and wine in general, but not to
> confusion of head. . . . Why does Lady Holland always have that
> damned screen between the whole room and the fire? I, who bear cold
> no better than an antelope, was absolutely petrified. All the rest too,
> looked as if they were just unpacked, like salmon, from an ice-
> basket. . . . When she retired, I watched their looks as I dismissed the
> screen, and every cheek thawed, and every nose reddened with the
> anticipated glow.
>
> At present I stand tolerably well with all. . . Holland's is the first—
> everything *distingué* is welcome there, and certainly the *ton* of his
> society is the best. Miladi in perfect good humour, and consequently
> *perfect*. No one more agreeable, or perhaps so much so, when she
> will.

By the end of its first decade the salon of Holland House already had
an unrivalled reputation. Both during the peace of 1814 and after
Waterloo, many eminent foreigners were regular visitors, among
them Mme. de Staël and her friend Baron von Humboldt, the
naturalist and traveller; General Lafayette; Count Pozzo di Borgo,
a roving diplomat of Corsican origin, a man of immense charm and
ability, who was, in turn, Russian Envoy to Paris and to London;
Count de Flahaut, natural son of Talleyrand; Sebastiani, the
Napoleonic general; the sculptor Antonio Canova; the Duc
d'Orléans; and the Portuguese statesman, Count Palmella.

There is little doubt that Holland House would have lost
something of its charm and magnetism without the presence of that
triumvirate of native wits—Sydney Smith, Henry Luttrell and
Samuel Rogers; to which Sydney Smith added a fourth name—that
of Sir James Mackintosh, who "with a few bad qualities added to his

PRUDENCE HANNAY

character would have acted a most conspicuous part in life."
Mackintosh's wit and learning reminded Greville of Burke and
Johnson, although the diarist considered himself to be more
agreeable than either of them. Greville said, though, that
Mackintosh was "probably equally instructive and amusing. I do not
know a greater treat than to hear him talk."

Henry Luttrell, the "most epigrammatic" talker Byron had ever
met, and the pleasantest companion Greville knew, found Holland
and Gore House equally agreeable. Samuel Rogers, though he was
a prominent host in his own right, spent much of his existence
under Lady Holland's wing. He was cadaverous, witty and
sometimes a viperish gossip; "next to the Congreve rocket," wrote
Sydney Smith, "he is the most mischievous and powerful of modern
inventions." Sydney Smith himself, cleric and man of letters, was
particularly devoted to Lady Holland, of whose foibles he had a
shrewd, instinctive grasp; in 1819, George Ticknor, a young
American tourist, delightfully portrayed his character:

> The house to which I went most frequently in London and where I
> spent a part of many evenings was Lord Holland's; and certainly for an
> elegant literary society I have seen nothing better in Europe. Lord
> Holland himself is a good scholar and a pleasant man in conversation;
> Sir James Mackintosh was staying at his house. Sydney Smith and
> Brougham came down there very often, and Heher (the book
> collector) and Frere, Lord Lansdowne, Lord Lauderdale, Lord
> Auckland, Lord John Russell, etc., and I do not well know how dinners
> and evenings could be more pleasant.
>
> Sydney Smith was in one respect the soul of the society. I never saw
> a man so formed to float down the stream of conversation and without
> seeming to have any direct influence upon it, to give it his own hue and
> charm. Notwithstanding the easy grace and light playfulness of his wit
> which comes forth with unexhausted and inexhaustible facility, yet he
> is a man of much culture and plain good sense, a sound, discreet
> judgment, and remarkably just and accurate habits of reasoning. This
> is a union of opposite qualities such as nature usually delights to hold
> asunder and such as makes him whether in company or alone an
> irresistibly amusing companion.

Lord Holland described Sydney's brother Bobus, one of his closest
friends, as "a library in himself, and when asked for a passage,
always had it at his tongue's end, and twenty others perhaps on the
same subject."

The Prince Regent and his brothers, the Dukes of York,
Clarence and Sussex, were all on visiting terms with the Hollands;

LADY HOLLAND

and the bond was strengthened when, in 1824, Charles Richard Fox married Lady Mary FitzClarence, daughter of the Duke of Clarence and the actress Mrs. Jordan. From 1820 onwards, under a new reign which had brought the possibility of sweeping political changes, Lord Holland acted as Lord Grey's aide in the Whig hierarchy. Evenings at Holland House acquired an increasingly political hue and, on the resignation of Lord Liverpool in 1827, came hopes of Whig supremacy at last; but they were dashed, though Canning and his successor Goderich both made overtures to Lord Holland, who promised his support but declined to take office, thus greatly disappointing Lady Holland. She had not long to wait, however, because, with the Whigs' return to power in November 1830, Lord Holland accepted the office of Chancellor of the Duchy of Lancaster in Lord Grey's Cabinet.

Holland House now entered upon its last and greatest phase. The new members of government were doubly welcome to Lady Holland—the Lords Althorp, Melbourne, Durham, Palmerston and Lansdowne, together with Lord John Russell, Sir James Graham, Charles Grant and Stanley. Cabinet dinners now took place regularly in Kensington; and on those occasions Lady Holland dined at Little Holland House but rejoined the company later in the evening. William IV, though averse to dining at private houses in London on the grounds of Royal etiquette, saw no reason to forego that pleasure in the country, for so he regarded Kensington. Thus, within the first weeks of his reign, he visited his daughter's relations; Lady Holland assembled for dinner the Dukes of Sussex and Argyll, Lord George Cavendish, the Lords Carlisle and Granville and their ladies (daughters of the beautiful Duchess of Devonshire), Lord Melbourne, Admiral Sir Thomas Hardy of Nelson fame, Henry Luttrell, Lady Affleck (Lady Holland's mother) and her sister-in-law, Miss Caroline Fox.

Among those who received regular invitations to Holland House at the beginning of the new decade were the two famous bachelor peers, the Duke of Devonshire and Lord Alvanley; Henry Hallam and Charles Greville; Augustus Calcott, David Wilkie and Sir Martin Archer Shee, who became President of the Royal Academy of 1830; the Lords Clanricarde and Cowper and their wives; Sir Francis Burdett, John Cam Hobhouse, the Lords Lyndhurst and Abinger; Lord and Lady William Russell; and the poets Thomas Moore and Thomas Campbell. During the same decade, the names of Thomas Babington Macaulay, Charles Dickens and Edwin

PRUDENCE HANNAY

Landseer were added to the list.

Foreign diplomats and dignitaries vied with each other for invitations; to be included on the visiting list to Holland House was now regarded as the height of social, and often of diplomatic, success. Heading foreign envoys to the Court of St. James's was the French Ambassador, Prince Talleyrand, the seventy-six-year-old statesman, who regarded Lady Holland's insistence on dining at five, when a later hour was almost universally appointed, as a deliberate act of defiance *"pour gêner tout le monde."* Nevertheless, he attended; and, despite his somewhat unattractive appearance in old age, Lady Holland was among the many who succumbed to his brilliance as a raconteur. Indeed, she believed him still to be the best story-teller in Europe. Other ambassadorial personages often seen at Holland House were Prince and Princess Lieven from Russia; Prince Esterhazy and Baron von Bülow from Austria and Prussia; Monsieur Dedel and Monsieur van der Weyer, representing Holland and Belgium respectively; and a very old friend, the Portuguese Count Palmella. In 1835 Talleyrand, by then an octogenarian, retired; and Prince Lieven, who had been recalled to Russia, was replaced by Count Pozzo di Borgo who, Lady Holland reported, "tells everybody the only *pleasure* he looks to is the *causerie* at Holland House."

It was during this decade that Charles Greville described the salon in his diary as "the house of all Europe":

> Such is the social despotism [he wrote] of this strange house, which presents an odd mixture of luxury and constraint, of enjoyment physical and intellectual with an alloy of small *désagréments* . . . Though everybody who goes there finds something to abuse or ridicule in the mistress of the house or its ways, all continue to go; all like it more or less; and whenever by the death of either it shall come to an end, a vacuum will be made in society which nothing will supply. It is the house of all Europe; the world will suffer by the loss and it may with truth be said that it will eclipse the gaiety of nations.

Macaulay, after his first introduction in 1831, became a regular habitué. Lady Holland herself was dazzled by his fund of historical knowledge and his descriptive powers; Greville, however, thought he lacked variety, elasticity and gracefulness: "His is a roaring current, and not a meandering stream of talk. I believe we would all of us have been glad to exchange some of his sense for some of Sydney's nonsense."

LADY HOLLAND

Charles Dickens was introduced by Serjeant Talfourd in 1837; though, unlike Lady Blessington to whom it was of no importance, Lady Holland had first enquired of Bulwer Lytton whether he were "presentable." She found him "modest and well-behaved"; and Lord Holland described him as "unobtrusive, yet not shy; intelligent in countenance and altogether prepossessing." But Dickens never felt quite so much at ease there as he did at Gore House; Lady Holland's quizzing often disarmed him against his better judgment, and he was even inveigled into revealing the plot of 'Nicholas Nickleby' long before the final installments had appeared. He would have heartily agreed with Talleyrand that "Lady Holland is all assertion".

As a political hostess during this period, Lady Holland was of immense service to the Whig Party; Gifford declared that "happy would be the day for their opponents if they could get up a Holland House on the Tory side of the question."

George Ticknor, lately retired from a professorship at Harvard, dined frequently with the Hollands, and wrote of the first occasion in 1835:

> I dined at Lord Holland's in his venerable and admirable establishment at Holland House. The party was small but select . . . Mr. Allen, Colonel Fox and his wife, Lord Grey, Lord Melbourne—the Premier himself; Mr. Labouchère, Lord and Lady Cowper and Lord Minto . . . The conversation was extremely vivacious and agreeable; Lord Grey, though seventy-one years old, talked well on subjects that came up, including Horace; Fanny Kemble's book which he cut to pieces without ceremony; the great question of the ballot and its application to English elections, etc . . . Lord Melbourne seemed to be very heartily liked by everybody. He too, was full of literary anecdote, and pleasant, frank and extremely easy talk, occasionally marked with a quick penetrating glance which showed him to be always ready and vigilant . . . Public business was much talked about—the Corporation Bill, the motion for admitting dissenters to the Universities, etc. Nothing could exceed the luxury of the recherché dinner, the conversation during the whole evening being very various and lively, much filled with literary allusion and spirit.

In 1834 Greville had noted a similar evening's talk, when the company included Spring Rice and his son, Lords Melbourne and Palmerston, Dr. Allen and Bobus Smith:

> There was a great deal of very good talk, anecdotes, literary criticism and what not . . . They talked of Taylor's new poem, "Philip van

PRUDENCE HANNAY

Artevelde"; Melbourne had read and admired it. They held Wordsworth cheap, except Spring Rice who was enthusiastic about him. Holland thought Crabbe the greatest genius of modern poets. Melbourne said he degraded every subject. None of them had known Coleridge; his lectures were very tiresome, but he is a poet of great merit. Then they spoke of Spencer Perceval and Irving preaching in the streets . . . After dinner they discussed women's works; few *chefs-d'oeuvres;* Madame de Sevigné, the best; the only three of a high class are Mme. de Sevigné, Mme. de Staël and (Bobus Smith said) Sappho; these however are unrivalled tho' Lady Holland would not hear of Mme. de Staël. They agreed as to Miss Austen that her novels are excellent . . . Of the early English kings there is no reason to believe that any king before Edward III understood the English language . . .

Lord Holland died in October 1840; but, after the initial shock, Lady Holland continued to entertain, for company had long been absolutely essential to her equilibrium. She herself died in November 1845, by which time many of her old friends had predeceased her—Sydney and Bobus Smith, Dr. Allen, Sir James Mackintosh, Joseph Jekyll, Lord Cowper, Sir Humphrey Davy. Queen Victoria wrote a note of sympathy to her old and dear friend Lord Melbourne, on hearing of Lady Holland's death. He replied:

Lord Melbourne presents his humble duty to Your Majesty, and thanks Your Majesty much for your letter of the 28th ult., which he received yesterday morning . . . . Lady Holland's death will be a great loss to many and Lord Melbourne is not only ready but anxious to admit that it will be so to him. The advantage of her house was that she asked almost everybody and thus it effected an opportunity of seeing persons whom one wished to see and whom one had no chance of seeing anywhere else. Lord Melbourne always found her a very kind, anxious, attentive and active Friend . . .

In the last analysis, Francois Guizot and Charles Greville reached a similar conclusion—that Lord Holland, for all his endearing qualities, was in the end, a lightweight; it was Lady Holland who possessed more heart.

FANNY VON ARNSTEIN

Open House in Vienna

Hilde Spiel

Some mortals are placed, as though by chance, at an important point along the river of time, at which it changes its course or is joined by an important tributary. Although the woman whose story is told here never directly influenced the progress of ideas or events, she was very conscious of the position she occupied and of the part that she could play, and fulfilled her role with intelligence, dignity and grace. Her life-span covered a period from the beginning of the Enlightenment to the return of reaction. When she died, her niece Lea, mother of the composer Felix Mendelssohn, mourned "the most interesting woman in Europe". This may have been exaggerated. Of the heroines of the German Emancipation around 1800 she was merely the first, and by no means the most highly gifted. She was not an intellectual like Rahel Varnhagen, not a Romantic reveller like Dorothea Schlegel, not the sentimental confidante of great minds like Henriette Herz. She was a social genius who knew how to please, to humour, to entertain, to stimulate, and who attracted some of her noblest, wittiest and most productive contemporaries. For more than three decades, she held open house in Vienna. Between the reign of the Emperor Joseph II and the Congress of Vienna and after, she received every person of talent and rank who lived in or visited the city.

Fanny von Arnstein herself, however, was a native of Berlin, the capital of Maria Theresa's life-long adversary and Germany's most enlightened monarch, Frederick the Great. Her father, Daniel Itzig, had been master of the Royal mint; and by the time Franziska married Nathan Adam Arnsteiner, son of the Court merchant of the late Emperor Francis the First, Itzig was one of the two Elders of the Jewish community, and the most influential man of his creed in Prussia. He lived splendidly at his palace in the Burgstrasse, facing King Frederick's castle, and in his mansion in the Köpenicker suburb, surrounded by large gardens that were surpassed only by the Royal park.

Franziska, the eighth of Daniel Itzig's children, had been as carefully brought up and well instructed in the arts as her sisters and her brothers. The Danish philosopher August von Hennings, when he visited Berlin in 1772, went to see not only the famous Moses Mendelssohn but also the banker Itzig. "He has sixteen children," Hennings wrote, "of whom some are already in independent positions, while others have just reached the age when beauty begins to unfold. The daughters' loveliness is enhanced by their talents, especially for music, and by their well-refined minds."

Of Itzig's eight daughters, it was most probably Franziska whose beauty he must have seen unfolding at the time. Her elder sisters— among them Bella, the future grandmother of Felix Mendelssohn— were already married, while the younger girls still lived in the nursery. Her musical talent, both as a singer and as a pianist, was to pave the way for her first social successes in Vienna, where she arrived in 1776 at the age of eighteen, a blue-eyed, slender, graceful girl, determined to surround herself with a circle no less advanced than her father's. But in the capital of the Holy Roman Empire, she found Jews were not treated with the comparative indulgence accorded to them in Frederick's Berlin. A hundred years earlier, they had been evicted from the city by the same Emperor Leopold whose taste and financial generosity helped to produce the magnificent buildings and musical masterpieces of the Austrian Baroque age. Later, because he needed money, he had permitted some to return; and, among these, Isaac Arnsteiner, the ancestor of Franziska's husband, had risen to a position of wealth and power. Yet Isaac's descendants continued to suffer restrictions and humiliations, even during the reign of the motherly Maria Theresa, who loathed all unconverted Jews with a fervour matched only by her Christian piety.

To a young woman fresh from Berlin, where, two decades earlier, Lessing and Nicolai had befriended Moses Mendelssohn and joined him in founding the editorial board of a humanist publication, and

HILDE SPIEL

where many writers were still engaged in furthering the cause of moral and religious reform, the atmosphere of comparative intolerance in Vienna must have seemed frustrating. Yet we find "Fanny" (as the Viennese soon were to call her) even before the Empress's death, attending and taking part in a musical soirée at the house of a Minister, von Hochstedten. That evening Mozart's former sweetheart and future sister-in-law, Aloysia Weber, is reported to have enchanted everyone with her singing, while "Frau von Arnstein"—politely and prematurely ennobled—"played the piano to our delight."

About the same time, she was first seen in the company of Caton von Preissing, the wife of the Court Secretary Obermayer, a young woman of her own age, who, until her early death, was to be Fanny's intimate friend. Despite the hostile attitude of the Throne, aristocrats and high civil servants in Vienna no longer closed their doors to Jewish people of breeding and wealth; and Fanny Arnstein was to take advantage of these tentative beginnings. Indeed, it was she who broke down the barriers and helped others following in her wake. "The free and honoured position, liberated from the burden of prejudice, which, in later days and up to now, people of the Mosaic faith were able to enjoy in Vienna, was undoubtedly gained by Frau von Arnstein's penetrating influence alone." Thus wrote the husband of Rahel Levin, August Varnhagen von Ense, in a portrait of Fanny written many years after her death.

How then did she succeed in overcoming her difficulties? Her early attempts can be traced in contemporary writings, from which it emerges that she was a friend of Joseph von Sonnenfels, the baptized Jew and great social reformer, well-loved by Maria Theresa once he changed his creed; that she attended Mozart's subscription concerts in the mixed company of Austrian noblemen, courtiers and rich Jewish converts; and that she presently won the esteem and admiration of what was then Vienna's literary elite. It is even known that she visited the Emperor Joseph, soon after his accession, to plead for her people while he was preparing his famous "Patent of Tolerance".

After the Patent had been issued in 1782, lifting many, though by no means all, restrictions imposed on the Jews in the Habsburg Empire, Fanny gradually assumed a recognized role in Austrian society. In the reminiscences of Franz Graeffer, a Viennese chronicler, she is described, during the third year of Joseph's reign, 1783, as a "highly educated woman, whose opinions were rightly considered to be worth as much as, and indeed, more than those of a whole academy," and who was "greeted and addressed by the Emperor whenever he caught sight of her." However euphemistic this praise may be, it is evident that Fanny appeared not only learned—which up to a point she was—but also a shrewd and penetrating judge. Her conversation, at least, must have matched her physical attractions and social grace.

In the early 1790s, during the short reign of Joseph's even more high-minded brother Leopold and that of his obscurantist nephew Francis, her salon seems to have been firmly established in her apartments on the Graben, a fashionable thoroughfare in the heart of Vienna. There she received a great number of distinguished visitors, while her regular guests and friends included two princes of Liechtenstein, the Russian Prince Czernitchev, Austrian aristocrats, several high court officials and two clerics—a remarkable array, especially in Franciscan Vienna, which was fast reverting to its previous prejudices and taboos. Fanny Arnstein, however, had made good use of the wind of change which had blown so favourably during Joseph's reign; and her personal accomplishments were sufficiently great to enable her to hold her ground; indeed, so powerful was her charm that the elder of the princes of Liechtenstein, a married man, fell in love with her and, on her account, fought a duel in which he lost his life.

Though her appearance might perhaps not have dazzled us, she was considered highly attractive by her contemporaries. Varnhagen says:

> Tall and slender, radiant with beauty and grace, of elegant manner and tone, of vivacious and fiery expressions, combining a sharp mind and wit with a gay dispostion, well-read and a master of foreign languages as well as of her own, she was almost striking and strange phenomenon in Vienna. Attributes few women in high society possessed were noticed with wonder in a Jewish woman whose refinement and freedom of spirit, nurtured by the beneficial influences of Frederick the Second's reign, seemed all the more effective in a city where these virtures scarcely existed, but where they had begun to be desired and to be esteemed.

From Berlin, which she visited frequently, Fanny brought back news of the latest books and ideas, which were avidly received both by Vienna's high-born dilettantes and by authors who took their cues from the great German school of writing. Travellers from all over Europe, such as the Schopenhauer family or Friedrich von Gentz, who was later to become an Austrian statesman and the Secretary General of the Congress of Vienna, called at Fanny's house. It was, as the saying went, "a case not of *who* one was, but *what* one was, in order to gain admission." Thus a salon flourished that was more permanent, much wider in social range and, finally, far more splendid than those established in Fanny's native Berlin by Henriette Herz and Rahel Levin.

It must be admitted that Nathan Arnstein, whose riches provided for his wife's copious, even luxurious hospitality, was not considered the soul of wit or a highlight of cultural accomplishment. An able businessman, well liked by everyone, he never shone in the company Fanny kept for anything except his goodness. He generously overlooked the affair that led to Prince Liechtenstein's death, preferred a quiet card game to the stress of brilliant talk, and won great esteem in his own world, that of merchant-banking. Yet, when the Emperor Francis chose to make him a baron of Austria and of the Holy Roman Empire, he did so in consideration of the "truly noble manners, reason, virtues and many praiseworthy accomplishments which our dear and faithful wholesale-merchant Nathan Adam Arnsteiner is famous for possessing."

Apart from their sumptuous town residence, the Arnsteins now owned an estate in a suburb that today forms part of the Viennese district of Hietzing. It included a summer palace that had formerly belonged to an archduchess, as well as extensive gardens, where Fanny tried to imitate the beautiful park of her father's property in Köpenick. There, in 1800, she received a famous Englishman, as we learn from the Weimar actress Caroline Jagemann's somewhat sarcastic description:

> In their [the Arnsteins'] very lovely domicile one could daily see foreigners from every country, and Lord Nelson with Lady Hamilton, known for her airs, was also expected. After many hours of uncertainty whether these illustrious people would accept the invitation, at last they arrived: Nelson, a slim small man with one eye and one arm, who did not look the hero, Lady Hamilton, a tall stately figure with the head of a Pallas, following him with his hat under her arm. They stayed the whole evening and left their hosts in the greatest satisfaction over the honour paid to them.

Another celebrated guest, Germaine de Staël, arrived in 1808; besides attending the less interesting but more exalted entertainments of the Princesses de Ligne, Liechtenstein and Lubomirski, or the Countesses Wrbna and Zamoiska, Madame de Staël occasionally put in an appearance at Fanny's salon. "Madame de Staël is in Vienna," wrote Rahel Varnhagen rather spitefully to a friend, "I would almost say with Frau von Arnstein." But, however inferior Fanny's standing might be, she was still the only former commoner, and a Jewess to boot, in the committee of a "Society of aristocratic ladies for the advancement of good and useful aims," that had been founded in 1811. When, after the fall of Napoleon (whom she despised notwithstanding his tolerant attitude towards the Jews, who were accorded full civil rights wherever he set foot in Europe), the great Congress of Vienna took place, Fanny's salon became the centre of social and political activities.

In the three establishments she owned in 1814—a house on the Hoher Markt, her estate in Hietzing and a country-house in Baden near Vienna—the assemblies she held were so brilliant that Rahel Varnhagen and her husband were astonished. "Persons of the highest rank and the most excellent importance," recorded Karl August von Varnhagen, "frequented her receptions. On any one evening you could meet in the throng the Duke of Wellington, the Cardinal Consalvi, the Prince of Hardenberg, the Counts Capo d'Istria and Pozzo di Borgo, the Baron Humboldt, the Prince of Hessen-Homburg, the Counts of Berndorff, of Munster and of Neipperg, and many of similar esteem." Her musical soirées, held every Tuesday night throughout the Congress, drew connoisseurs as well as diplomats, statesmen and members of all the reigning European Houses excepting only their crowned heads. Once, when it proved too small, her husband hired a large ballroom, to give a particularly splendid entertainment.

It was in Fanny's salon, too, that the first Christmas tree was seen in Vienna; and its importation from Prussia was noted sneeringly by the Austrian secret police: "The day before yesterday, at the Arnsteins, a much frequented Christmas tree celebration was held according to Berlin practice. There were the State Chancellor Hardenberg, the State Councillors Jordan and Hoffmann, Prince Radzivill, Herr Bartholdy, all the baptized and circumsized relations of the house." The Baroness von Arnstein herself had never been and was never to be baptized. Unlike the other heroines of the Jewish emancipation, Dorothea Mendelssohn, Rahel Levin, Henriette Herz, Marianne Eybenberg among them, she remained faithful to the creed of her fathers. She alone of her famous

HILDE SPIEL

generation, when she died in 1818, was buried according to ancient rites and laid to rest in the Jewish cemetery, in a sarcophagus that stands today amid a wilderness of weeds and broken tombstones.

Fanny had not avoided baptism for bigoted reasons. Throughout her life, she had been a pupil of Moses Mendelssohn, a firm believer in the theory of the equality of all religions, as symbolized by the "Fable of the Three Rings" in G. E. Lessing's play *Nathan the Wise* (whose model Mendelssohn himself was). Because she believed that all faiths were equal before God, she did not object to her only daughter Henriette's conversion. It was this daughter, wife of a Sephardic Jew, Baron Pereira, and mother of four sons, all married into the high Austrian aristocracy, who carried on Fanny's tradition after her death. During the more modest Biedermeier period, Henriette attracted to her Friday receptions such eminent contemporaries as the writers Grillparzer, Stifter and Prince Friedrich Schwarzenberg, as well as the painters Schwind, Schnorr and Amerling. Her salon, fondly described by Stifter and commemorated in the diaries of her friend Ottilie von Goethe, was one of the few centres of Austrian cultural activity before the revolution of 1848.

Unlike Rahel Varnhagen, whose large collection of letters as well as reports of aphorisms, witticisms and philosophic utterances have been handed down to us, Fanny left next to nothing—a number of testaments, a small notebook with quotations from her favourite authors, a few remarks. We can only guess how she impressed her contemporaries by some isolated description, as when she was called "a wondrous picture," "a queen of all festive gatherings," a "magic woman," or else, "scandalously Prussian" and a "beautiful Hebrew". Perhaps it is more important we should know that, after her, in Varnhagen's words, "no lady of her kind penetrated into the circle of the high nobility," and that her position was achieved "through many years of self-reliance in dignity and splendour, through great charity and social activities, allied with spiritual courage and notable wisdom of the world."

When Fanny first entered society, gentile and male dominance were melting away beneath the light of Reason. But the great era of the Enlightenment, if only in Central Europe, was already doomed. With the rise of the Romantic age, represented by the brothers Grimm, Achim von Arnim, Clemens Brentano and others, irrational forces again came to the fore and political reaction set in. Not long after Fanny's death, anti-Semitic slogans were shouted by

FANNY VON ARNSTEIN

students who belonged with the new Germanic and nationalist movement; and still darker times lay ahead. Even so, what had been once achieved could not be lost forever. Not by deeds, but by the sheer example of her mode of being, Fanny had given proof that human qualities might have an absolute value beyond the boundaries of sex and creed.

HILDE SPIEL

MADAME RÉCAMIER

A Romantic French Salon

Cynthia Gladwyn

After the Restoration of Louis XVIII in 1815, one of the most distinguished Parisian salons was that of Juliette Récamier, whose celebrated admirer, the great romantic, François René de Chateaubriand dominated every gathering; and it was here that the first chapters of his immortal *Mémoires d'Outre Tombe* were read aloud to a delighted audience.

The hostess herself did not pretend to be an intellectual, nor was she particularly quick-witted; but she possessed extraordinary tact and, above all, a gift for listening. Her kind disposition, that rare but winning quality, was an added charm. Yet, although she had an immense capacity for love, she completely lacked the flame of passion. She was, nevertheless, an outrageous coquette, and often encouraged flirtatiousness in others.

Jeanne Françoise Julie Adelaïde Bernard, an only child, had been born on December 3, 1777, at Lyons, where her father was a notary. From her mother she inherited her looks but not her temperament, which, it is said, was typically Lyonnais. According to Renan, the women of Lyons have "delicate decency" together with "voluptuous chastity" and "seductive reserve". Madame Bernard was an attractive and ambitious woman, who cleverly managed her family's affairs; and, through the influence of one of her adorers, Charles de Calonne, Minister of Finance, her husband was appointed *Receveur des Finances* in Paris, whither the Bernards moved in 1774. At Lyons Juliette had had a convent education; but now her mother instilled in her the importance of femininity and the art of pleasing. Many of her mannerisms, which, later, were both praised and criticized, had been acquired in early youth. Tremendous trouble was taken over her appearance; she was present at all her mother's parties, and accompanied her everywhere. When, on the eve of the Revolution, she went to Versailles to see the King and Queen dine in public, the extreme elegance of Madame Bernard and her daughter was singled out by Marie Antoinette, who invited them to come afterwards to her own apartments; there Juliette was measured back-to-back with Madame Royale (later Duchesse d'Angoulème) to the keen annoyance of the latter, as they were just the same age. During the Revolution, Bernard escaped the guillotine through Madame Bernard's friendship with Barère de Vieuzac, President of the Convention. She continued to plan for her family; and, in 1793, at the age of fifteen, Juliette was married off to a rich Paris banker, the son of a Lyons hatter, whom she had known since childhood; but she continued to live with her mother for two years. Jacques Récamier, handsome, easy-going, pleasure-loving, was nearly twenty-seven years older than his bride. Their marriage was never consummated, a fact that gave rise to two theories, both almost certainly erroneous. Some believed that Récamier was her father, and that only by marrying her was it possible, at that time, to leave her his fortune; he certainly expected to be guillotined, since he regularly went to watch executions in order to accustom himself to his fate. This explanation seems unlikely though, judging from the deeply hurt letter that he wrote her in the year 1807. Anxious to marry again, she had asked for a divorce; and he reminds her how he had respected her susceptibilities and her dislike of normal marriage. This letter also refutes the alternative theory that she had some physical imperfection. Had this been so, she would hardly, in 1807, have thought of embarking on marriage with a man six years younger than herself.

In 1795 French life, under the Directoire, was marked by a wild outburst of extravagance and gaiety; and the fantastic fashions of the *Incroyables* and *Merveilleuses* were succeeded by classical modes and transparent décolleté dresses. Récamier's child-bride, once she had been handed over to him, became one of the leaders of this new society. She had blossomed into a lovely young woman, for whom her understandably unfaithful husband delighted in parading. He showered on her every luxury, and bought for her the

CYNTHIA GLADWYN

town-house that had once belonged to Jacques Necker, Louis XVI's Minister of Finance, in the rue du Mont Blanc; Récamier had redecorated it in the Directoire style and his wife held lavish entertainments there. Those were her frivolous years, when she danced all night, went to masked balls and slept all day. Callers would be told: "It isn't yet daylight with Madame." Enchantingly pretty rather than beautiful, she had a lithe figure, curly chestnut hair and a dazzling transparency of complexion seldom seen in Latin countries. Her unhurried movements and gentle manner contrasted with the animation of most Parisian *élégantes*. Her eyes were generally downcast; but, if she raised them, she would first turn them away from, and then toward the person she wished to charm, with a peculiarly captivating expression.

Invariably, she wore white, emblematic of her purity; dressed in diaphanous muslin, she would enter a room hesitant, blushing, timid. She alternated between diffidence and an almost roguish coquetry, and often encouraged her admirers to begin an amorous pursuit that she did not mean to satisfy, and which, in the end, she deftly but sweetly eluded. Yet, with two notable exceptions, Lucien Bonaparte and Benjamin Constant, the disappointed lover was magically converted into a devotee for life. Goethe makes Faust say that he staggers from desire to enjoyment, and that, at the height of enjoyment, he regrets the desire. Madame Récamier contrived to keep her adorers at that delightful stage, the opening of the love affair. Sainte-Beuve interprets it as a wish to make everything stop in April.

This dexterity seems to have developed when she met and charmed Napoleon's brother, Lucien Bonaparte, an unattractive man accustomed to easy conquests among women of a lower kind. Naming himself Romeo, he was the first to pursue Juliette seriously. Perplexed by his lengthy love letters and determined attack, she would have preferred to shut her doors against him; but Récamier, though he praised his wife's virtue, was exceedingly embarrassed. General Bonaparte's brother was far too important to rebuff; Récamier foresaw possible financial ruin. He begged her, therefore—without giving in—on no account to discourage him. Thus, Lucien was kept at bay for a year, when he finally gave up. But he had his revenge. Finding himself next to her at a banquet, he rose to toast the most beautiful woman in the world. Juliette looked suitably modest, and was then confused when he raised his glass "to Peace".

MADAME RÉCAMIER

When Lady Bessborough, sister to Georgina, Duchess of Devonshire, and one of the most fascinating women of her time, was in Paris during the brief Peace of Amiens in 1802, she wrote to her lover, Lord Granville Leveson Gower (the future Earl Granville) giving her impressions of the famous Madame Récamier; she had heard the French say of her *"Elle n'est galante que de buste"*, and added, apropos of the witticism, "Don't be shocked but hide your face when you recall it, as I have for an hour. . ." She had attended a ball given by Juliette, she told him, in the middle of which the latter "literally went to bed and let anybody come to look at her." This, apparently, was by no means unusual. Sometimes Juliette would retire from her party to have a good cry; for, despite all her triumphs, she had a melancholy nature. Two days later, Lady Bessborough again describes

> how distressed I was at Madame Récamier's. We went there and found her in bed—that beautiful bed you saw prints of—muslin and gold curtains, great looking-glasses at the side, incense pots, etc and muslin sheets trimmed with lace, and beautiful white shoulders expos'd perfectly uncovered to view—in short completely undressed and in bed. The room was full of men . . . and she explained to the whole company that she was not with child.

In 1814 Lady Bessborough was back in Paris and once more described going "at ten to Mad Récamier's to meet Mad de Staël and Benjamin Constant". As before, the hostess was in bed, "without a night cap . . . and having *la fièvre* she had taken something to make her perspire; the number of people in the room no doubt assisted the effect of the medicine very much". Sometimes the room was so crowded that people stood on chairs to see; whereupon their host sent for napkins to protect his silken covers. Her behaviour was not a form of exhibitionism, but the naive innocence of a woman who, says Henri de Latouche, was "so virginal that he hesitated to call her Madame"; and it was this quality that protected her from scandal. There was criticism, certainly. Some said that her little mannerisms were affected; that the Madonna-like pose of blue eyes gazing heavenward, with the mouth slightly open, was held too long, and the coquetry was more like that of a *grisette* than of a lady. While the peace lasted, she made a triumphal visit across the Channel to see her English friends. On May Day, when fashionable society flocked to Kensington Gardens, she caused a sensation by wearing a bonnet with a white

CYNTHIA GLADWYN

veil that encircled her to the ground. Her admirers said that people had gone down on their knees before her; but, in fact, they were trying to lift her veil to glimpse the face about which they had heard so much. French émigrés still in England were sarcastic about this exaggerated fashion set by the wife of a hatter.

For Juliette the acquistion of the house in the rue du Mont Blanc had opened up a new vista. Negotiations had been conducted through Necker's daughter, Germaine de Staël, who found her charming; and a lasting friendship was established. The brilliant, dominating Madame de Staël adopted the position of an affectionate elder sister, and set Juliette on a more interesting path in life. With her Juliette met the intelligentsia, and they too joined her salon. She made friends with the Montmorencys, a celebrated family of the *ancienne noblesse*, who, because of their enlightened ideas, had been cold-shouldered by the other émigrés. Adrien (later, Duc de Laval) became an ambassador of credit after the restoration of the Bourbons; Mathieu (later, Duc de Montmorency) had been the lover of Madame de Staël. But now, deeply religious, he was prepared to worship a virginal beauty; and the two formed the adoring nucleus of Juliette's receptions. Then the great generals were invited; and the First Consul demanded "Since when has the Council met at Madame Récamier's?" When Madame de Staël openly criticized the Napoleonic regime and was exiled, Madame Récamier also fell under suspicion. She had refused to become a lady-in-waiting to Josephine, and she received guests who were Napoleon's enemies. Her husband's bank then failed, and the state refused assistance. The Récamiers were forced to sell everything and live modestly, a disaster that she accepted with calm resignation.

To help Juliette recover from this crisis, Germaine de Staël invited her to Coppet, her *château* on the Lake of Geneva whither she had retired, and where many of her friends gathered. Juliette arrived in the summer of 1807, after a bad carriage accident on an Alpine road that had killed two horses and injured her foot—the place, said the devout Mathieu, should be marked with a cross. Something that alarmed him even more befell Juliette at Coppet. She was attracted by a twenty-four-year-old Prussian Prince, Augustus of Prussia, the nephew of Frederick the Great and the father of two illegitimate children. This dashing and handsome young man came to stay, fell violently in love and proposed marriage. Their hostess encouraged the affair; she reminded

Juliette, who now had "reduced" her age by two years, that she still had the right to wear the bridal wreath of orange-blossom. Largely at the instigation of Madame de Staël, Juliette asked her husband for a divorce; and meanwhile she had some romantic moments on Lake Geneva with the Prince. Although deeply pained, Récamier agreed to the divorce, but begged that Juliette's marriage take place abroad. She thought of suicide, but eventually renounced the Prince, with (at least one of her biographers suspects) a certain sense of relief; and she behaved badly by not letting him know for some months—because she hesitated to hurt his feelings—that all was definitely over.

Juliette herself was, at length, exiled from Paris; she had been identified too closely with Madame de Staël; and her friends included the generals Moreau and Bernadotte, who defected from Napoleon. She spent much time at Lyons, then revisited Coppet and travelled to Italy. By now she had adopted Récamier's young niece, who became Madame Lenormant and, after her death, edited Juliette's *Souvenirs et Correspondance*, suppressing all that she considered unsuitable for posterity. Juliette's first meeting with the man whose admiration would immortalize her took place in Paris in 1801. He had gone one morning to see Madame de Staël, who held forth with her usual brilliance. But Chateaubriand scarcely heard a word. Into the room had walked an exquisite figure in white, who sat on a blue silk sofa and listened, and later slipped away. Not until 1817 did he meet her again. Madame de Staël had had a stroke, and liked her friends to dine without her while she lay paralyzed in the next room and occasionally joined in the conversation. Juliette and Chateaubriand hardly spoke until the end of the meal, at which point she turned to him, beautiful in her distress for the dying Germaine. He describes how he looked up and saw his guardian angel. The Enchanter had found the Sylph whom he had dreamed of since his boyhood. Sainte-Beuve has some sound advice for women. Do not, he says, fall in love with Voltaire, Rousseau, Goethe or Chateaubriand. Love the man who offers you his entire heart. Glory, as a third party in the *tête-à-tête*, spoils everything.

François René, vicomte de Chateaubriand, was born in 1769. A Celt from the wild shore of St. Malo, he had been brought up in the romantic Château de Combourg, full of ghosts and legends and mysteries. Restless and melancholy, he had grown to love nature, and, wandering in the woods, had enjoyed dreams of his ideal

CYNTHIA GLADWYN

woman. At seventeen he had crossed the Atlantic, but had returned from America in 1791 to fight against Revolutionary France with the Royalist army. For this he needed money; and his family had arranged his marriage to a woman who proved to be the antithesis of his Sylph and by no means rich. She was plain, full of common sense, unromantic, and, according to her husband, never read his works. Having been wounded, he found his way to England, where he taught in a Suffolk boarding school, and then lodged with an erudite clergyman with whose daughter he fell in love. Though attraction was mutual, he was obliged to confess that he was married, and fled from the house, leaving his luggage behind.

He now began to write, and returned to France in 1800 with the manuscript of *Le Génie du Christianisme*, which was acclaimed as a masterpiece two years later; its publication happened luckily to coincide with the re-establishment of the Catholic religion in France. After the judicial murder of the Duc d'Enghien in 1804, Chateaubriand turned against Napoleon, comparing him to Nero. The author was short and broad-shouldered with a magnificent head; his hair was disheveled as though he were still on the coast of Brittany, and he had flashing eyes, a melancholy expression and an irresistible smile.

In the autumn of 1818 the Enchanter and the Sylph were both at a country-house at Chantilly, where a terrace opened onto a mysterious wood. Here they wandered together in the evenings; and there must have been some idyllic love-making, the extent of which can only be surmised. The malicious made jokes about this affair—for example, that "she could not receive what he could not give". Their letters, however, which were intercepted by the Secret Police on the orders of Louis XVIII, with whom Chateaubriand was now on bad terms, are full of references to these meetings in the glades, and of entreaties that they should never be forgotten. The following spring Juliette wrote what is believed to be her only extant love letter: "I love you less?. . . No more does it depend on me, nor on you, nor on anybody to prevent me from loving you; my love, my life, my heart—all are yours." Whether this letter establishes the consummation of their love affair is perhaps doubtful, coming, as it did, from the virginal woman who all her life declared: "I need to love and be loved, no matter by whom." Moreover, when Chateaubriand was old and widowed, Juliette offered to move into his house, saying that "the world knows how pure is our love for each other". She once confided to her niece that the only beautiful

MADAME RÉCAMIER

days of her life had been two weeks she had spent at Coppet with Prince Augustus, and the first two years of Chateaubriand's love; but the Prince had been too passionate.

Worshippers at Madame Récamier's shrine were horrified by the arrival in their midst of this remarkable man, who disturbed the harmony of the salon, monopolized her attention, and behaved as though he were master of the house. One of the faithful, the religious writer Simon Ballanche, warned her that Chateaubriand "was intoxicated with himself like all despotic rulers", and suggested that she translate Plutarch into French verse to divert her thoughts. But his warning had no effect. What appealed to her in Chateaubriand was that, for the first time, she had met a man who, instead of being interested in her, insisted on her being interested in him.

In 1819 Récamier had his last financial crisis; and his wife moved alone to a small, simple apartment with brick floors, in a convent on the Left Bank, the Abbaye-aux-Bois. Here she re-opened her salon. Having climbed three steep flights, Chateaubriand arrived breathless, but enchanted with what he called her cell. From the open window the setting sun gilded a magnificent view, with the hills of Sèvres in the distance. Juliette was playing the piano and the Angelus was ringing.

There followed his diplomatic appointments to Berlin, to London, to the Congress of Verona as French Foreign Minister, and, of course, his continual love affairs. Madame Récamier now learned what it was to be jealous. During this period she even addressed him as Monsieur; and, in November 1823, she decided to make her absence felt. She left for Italy, where she remained nearly two years, escorted by Ballanche and a young historian, Jean Jacques Ampère, who had joined her circle. When she returned, her hair was white; though she preserved her looks to an advanced age, she said she knew that all was over when the little street urchins no longer turned round to stare. "Beauty," she wrote, "is a short tyranny."

Chateaubriand, again in favour with the Tuileries after the death of Louis XVIII, was in Rheims for the coronation of Charles X. As soon as he returned to Paris, without explanation or apology, he resumed his daily visits to the Abbaye. From then on, despite his love affairs, Juliette dedicated her life to warding off the attacks of boredom from which her "monarch" often suffered; and her salon achieved an unprecedented brilliance.

CYNTHIA GLADWYN

ahel Varnhagen von Ense;
s a young married woman, 1822. (1)

Karl August Varnhagen
von Ense, 1840. (2)

he salon: Heine plays tribute to the hostess, 1822. (3)

Lady Blessington and
Count d'Orsay at the
theatre; a contemporary
drawing. (4)

"The most elegant and best informed
woman" Landor had ever conversed with;
after a sketch by Landseer, 1830. (5)

Lord Blessington, Irish landowner
and roving dilettante;
after a portrait by d'Orsay. (6)

Opposite: Lady Blessington at the zenith of her beauty; portrait by Lawrence, c. 182

Lady Holland, painted at Florence in 1795 by Louis Gauffier. (8)

The Library at Holland House; the Hollands with their resident librarian, Dr. Allen. Painting by C. Leslie. (9)

land House, the south side. (10)

tte Récamier, as a leader of Parisian fashion,
'danced all night...and slept all day".
ait by Gérard. (11)

François René de Chateaubriand;
"intoxicated with himself like all
despotic rulers." Portrait by Deveria.
(12)

Medallion by David d'Angers;
"I need to love and be loved,
no matter by whom." (13)

Fanny von Arnstein. (14)

Prince von Liechtenstein
with his wife and son, 1792.
Passionately in love
with Fanny, the Prince
fought a duel on
her account that
cost him his life. (15)

Madame de Girardin; friend of the French Romantic poet, in whose salon Lamartine shone "with an incomparable brilliance". (16)

e Girardin; famous editor and celebrated amorist. (17)

Madame de Lieven, as ambassadress, confidante of sovereigns and politicians, and "one of the brightest luminaries of the London social world"; unfinished portrait by Lawrence. (18)

François Guizot, statesman and scholar, Madame de Lieven's last and greatest love. A daguerrotype of Guizot in old age. (19)

Prince Metternich, "Grand Inquisitor of Europe." (20)

A large apartment on the first floor, with great windows overlooking the garden, had recently become vacant; and there she arranged her rather shabby and now outmoded Directoire furniture, her harp, her piano and all her familiar belongings. One wall was dominated by the huge picture by Gérard of Madame de Staël as "*Corinne au Cap Misène*", which, when lit up by the sun, almost seemed to come to life. She was able to live in some style, with a footman to open the door. The chairs were placed in a circle that suited general conversation. Sometimes there were several circles. The armchair on the left of the fireplace, opposite the hostess, was reserved for Chateaubriand, and was protected from draughts by a Louis XV screen. He would arrive punctually at three o'clock—passers-by in the street set their watch by him—when he insisted on having an hour alone with his Sylph. They had *thé à l'anglaise* and *petit fours* together at four o'clock. Then the rest of the company was admitted. It was Madame Récamier who started the fashion of receiving at this hour; earlier than 1830, friends called in the evening. A chosen few would remain for dinner, which was a rather family affair with Chateaubriand, Monsieur and Madame Lenormant, and occasionally Récamier himself, until he died in 1830. The rule of the convent was that everybody had to be out by midnight. Juliette's guests called themselves "the Cinderellas".

Her smile of welcome was no longer flirtatious, but expressed sympathy and understanding; and she listened to what was said with deep interest. She spoke little, but always with tact and kindness, praising the talented, encouraging the shy, soothing the difficult. Faults of character were excused, as though they were symptoms of an incurable illness. She brought newcomers up to their friends, and took care that different coteries should be kept apart, a planned harmony that some disliked. But her salon, though mainly literary, now consisted of a wide variety of guests; for not only did she receive her old devotees, but politicians, the Faubourg St. Germain, artists and distinguished foreigners. When Mathieu de Montmorency, at Madame Récamier's urging, became an *Academicien*, her cell was known as the antechamber to the Academy. Sometimes there was music, or recitations by Talma, the renowned actor, and later the great actress Rachel. Latouche, now editor of a small newspaper, *Le Figaro*, read the works of an obscure and destitute poet, Madame Desbordes-Valmore, for whom Juliette obtained a pension.

Next, she thought of organizing readings from the works of

Chateaubriand. The first fragment of the *Mémoires d'Outre Tombe* was begun in 1809. The author had had an extrasensory experience, unusual for a Frenchman, though not perhaps for a Breton. The song of a thrush in the park of Monbuissier had suddenly and vividly swept him back to his youth in the woods of Combourg; and, when *Souvenirs d'enfance et de jeunesse* was read to an intimate group, both the writer and his audience wept. Then came another separation. Chateaubriand was appointed Ambassador to Rome in 1828; but this time he wrote by courier to his "beautiful angel" and implored her not to cry. In these letters, he said, he had "left the history of his secret feelings and of his private life during that period". He did not tell her of the amours with Roman beauties that perturbed his staff. Political events at home made him resign his successful ambassadorship the following year; but he failed to get the Ministry of Foreign Affairs for which he had been hoping. Juliette, who had felt abandoned and depressed, wrote to her niece that his return had brought her back to life again. To take his mind off politics, she at once arranged a reading of his tragedy *Moïse*. Lamartine reported that "all the glory and all the charm of France" were present. The tragedy was received with politeness, but with general disappointment; Madame Récamier was wretched at its failure.

After the July Revolution of 1830 and the accession of Louis-Philippe, Chateaubriand, loyal to the legitimate Bourbons, divested himself with a grand gesture of his title of Peer and Minister of State. He wished to be exiled; but as the King was too astute to make a martyr of him, he exiled himself by going with his wife to Switzerland. Here Juliette joined them for a while, and made a pilgrimage to the grave of Madame de Staël at Coppet. Chateaubriand's political life was over; but he had long been working on and revising his famous *Mémoires*, which were to be published only after his death. As he needed money, Juliette decided to arouse interest by having readings in her salon of the full text; and this was the moment of her greatest triumph. In February and March 1834, a distinguished gathering of only fifteen, the elite of Paris, came every day to the Abbaye at two o'clock. Chateaubriand brought his manuscript wrapped in a silk handkerchief, and, with attention and evident enjoyment, weighed every word as it was read by Ampère and Lenormant. He had an outstanding success. The daily papers and all the reviews were enthusiastic and clamoured for extracts; and a company was founded to provide him with a

CYNTHIA GLADWYN

large advance and an annuity. The comfort of his old age was assured.

The Chateaubriands now moved to the rue du Bac, only ten minutes' walk from the Abbaye; and Madame de Chateaubriand begged Madame Récamier not to leave Paris, even for a short time, as Chateaubriand was intolerable without her. She, therefore, found new interesting companions, organized more readings, did anything she could to keep him happy. But the pair were growing old, and their health was failing. Chateaubriand made two rash journeys. An ardent supporter of the legitimate Pretender to the Throne, the Comte de Chambord, Chauteaubriand crossed the Channel in November 1843 to pay the young man homage. While in England, he wandered through Kensington Gardens and thought of Juliette and her youthful beauty, and of himself, when he was an unknown émigré. Two years later, he again decided that he must see the King before he died, and made an exhausting expedition to Venice; but he broke his collar-bone in a carriage accident, and the injury affected him severely.

His legs were now paralyzed; he had to be carried up to the salon. His beautiful Sylph herself was ill and slowly going blind. Two operations were unsuccessful. When Madame de Chateaubriand died in 1847, Chateaubriand asked Juliette to marry him. She said that, had she been younger, she would not have refused; but she was wise enough to know that now he was happier anticipating his visits than if he were seeing her all day. When he could not come to the Abbaye, she arranged for friends to meet in the rue du Bac. But soon he fell silent and appeared to be in a dream. He could not speak to her; she could not see him. Chateaubriand was like an old oak struck by lightning, but "splendid in its ruin". The news that the Citizen King had been overthrown momentarily aroused him, as did the canonade of the revolution, the third he had witnessed, that broke out that summer of 1848. He died on July 4, with his Sylph praying at his bedside.

The proud Breton had left dramatic instructions for his burial. Surrounded by the sea he had loved all his life and which he called his "old mistress", he lies on a small rocky island in the bay of St. Malo, the Grand Bé. A granite cross and slab, but no name, mark the lonely grave.

Because of her failing eyesight Juliette now lived in darkened rooms. On entering, the visitor was guided only by her voice; and, if the door opened at the hour once consecrated to Chateaubriand,

MADAME RÉCAMIER

she gave a little shudder. The Comtesse d'Agoult, the blue-stocking and author, who had eloped with Franz Liszt, and who wished to write about Madame de Staël, was taken to the Abbaye in the spring of 1849. She describes the damp badly-lit staircase, and the blind Juliette, at last in black, graceful and slender with delicate pale features and, under her bonnet, a fringe of false brown hair. Her expression and way of speaking were gentle; and she paid her visitors flattering compliments. But she was firmly discreet about her old friend's love affairs, saying one should not touch on that side of her life. Madame d'Agoult found the celebrated hostess curiously uninteresting and untalented, hesitant in her speech and gestures, and with a schoolgirl's lack of poise. She was moved, however, when she heard Juliette say, "It is sad to grow old. One's memories become confused; but they remain as painful as ever."

Madame Récamier always dreaded cholera; and when, that Easter, it broke out in the rue de Sèvres, she moved to her niece's house near the Bibliothèque Nationale, where she continued to receive guests. Nevertheless, she was suddenly taken ill, and, after a night of agony, died the next morning on May 11, 1849. Her face had an angelic serenity. During the autumn of 1906 the Abbaye-aux-Bois was pulled down; and, while it was being dismantled, some interested visitors went to see the room where the famous salon had been held. An old nun remembered Juliette well, and knew all the important men who had climbed her stairs, though their names she had forgotten. But she clearly remembered the aged Monsieur de Chateaubriand, brought every afternoon by his servant, mounting the staircase with difficulty on his two sticks.

Madame Récamier was fortunate to live in a leisured age. Her peculiar appeal and the quality that Chateaubriand found most seductive, her gift of "associating herself with your existence", would have been lost in the hurly-burly of the modern world. Above all, she was fortunate in being loved by a man of genius who, though egotistic and unfaithful, had brought her lasting fame. She had "the double charm", he once wrote, "of the virgin and the woman who loves". Virginity has always had a mysterious and deep-rooted attraction for the human male.

CYNTHIA GLADWYN

MADAME DE GIRARDIN
The Tenth Muse

Joanna Richardson

On January 26, 1804, at Aix-la-Chapelle, Mme. Sophie Gay (née Lavalette) gave birth to a daughter, who was called Delphine. The infant, so the legend goes, was baptized on the tomb of Charlemagne. She was close to glory, from the first. Monsieur Gay was Receiver-General of Finance in the Rhenish provinces. Mme. Gay was a wit; and, alas, her wit cost her husband his place, with its revenue of 100,000 francs a year.

> Having one evening, in a public assembly, spoken satirically of the prefect of the department of which M. Gay was Receiver-General, she found herself, upon the following day, suddenly provided with passports for herself, her husband and five children (of whom Delphine was the youngest), and also with orders that none of the family should re-enter Aix, nor the ancient department to which it belongs.
>
> Furious at this mandate, Mme. Sophie Gay started off to Paris, and, failing when she reached the capital to obtain another appointment for her husband as valuable as that of which he was deprived, she is accused of having revenged herself by joining Madame Tallien in opposing the government and the Emperor Napoleon.
>
> Mme. Sophie Gay became a widow. It was then that she turned seriously to literature as a means of subsistence for herself and her children.

She wrote novels of French society under the Directoire and the Empire; but she still earned more renown for her conversation.

Indeed, she gathered around her in time the most distinguished writers of the Restoration, including Chateaubriand himself. Talma, Napoleon's favourite actor, came to her *salon* with Mlle. Duchesnois, the *tragédienne*. Carle Vernet, fresh from his easel, brought his son Horace, the future painter of battle scenes. "The company talked, laughed, danced, and gambled; for Mme. Sophie Gay, it is said, was a desperate player. But, whatever her faults, she was not jealous of her daughter, Delphine, who in the midst of this society grew up beautiful, graceful, modest, and a genius."

The term was used by Mrs. Challice, later in the century, when she wrote *French Authors at Home*. It may sound a Victorian extravagance; and yet, at fourteen, Delphine was reading her poetry aloud in her mother's salon. She was soon known as the Tenth Muse. Béranger praised the beauty of her shoulders, and Chateaubriand delighted in her smile. In 1822 she ventured to send the Académie-Française a poem about the sublime devotion of the sisters of St. Camilla to the sick and dying during the plague of Barcelona. Her choice of subject and her style won her Academic acclaim; and from the age of eighteen she was considered a Parisian celebrity. She contributed to *La Muse française*, the literary review which flourished in the early days of Romanticism. In 1824 she published her *Essais poétiques*, and the following year *Nouveaux Essais poétiques*. Her talent and, perhaps even more, her spirit and her beauty, made her the queen of the Romantic *cénacles*.

Legend says that there was a rumour of a morganatic marriage between Delphine and the Comte d'Artois (the future Charles X). But Delphine was certainly ignorant of such plans. The Comte d'Artois—who was forty-seven years her senior—was faithful to the memory of his mistress, Mme. de Polastron. After his accession to the throne, however, he received Delphine in audience. "Mademoiselle," he said to her:

> your poetic talent is of a very high order. From this day's date you will receive an annual pension of 500 crowns from my privy purse. This sum will enable you to travel. Inspiration, believe me, is to be found in a long journey, and there are dangers in Paris which I advise you to flee.

Mrs. Challice reports this conversation in her engaging book. However apocryphal it may be, Delphine set off with her mother through France, Switzerland and Italy, reciting her poems and charming society. Wherever she appeared, we are told, "there was

JOANNA RICHARDSON

an ovation to her talent and beauty; and in Italy she became so popular that, like another Corinne, she was crowned with laurels, and conducted in public triumph to the Capitol."

It was in Italy, in 1825, that Delphine first encountered one of the most significant figures in her life. Some chose to associate her with Alfred de Vigny, who in her Paris days was a handsome young officer in the royal bodyguard. Léon Séché, in his *Muses romantiques*, recorded that Alphonse de Lamartine was always to shine "with incomparable brilliance" in her heaven. Years later, after her death, Lamartine himself was to recall how he had first met her at the little village of Terni. She was sitting on a fallen treetrunk, holding a bunch of periwinkles, and she was gazing at the waterfall.

> Her profile, slightly aquiline, was like that of the women of the Abruzzi; she recalled them, too, by the energy of her build and by the gracious curve of her neck. This profile stood out brilliantly against the blue of the sky and the green of the waters; pride struggled there with sensibility; the brow was masculine, the mouth was feminine; the very mobile lips bore the impression of melancholy. . .
>
> We came back together to Terni; we parted there that evening, she to go to Rome, and I to return to Florence. She had left a gracious and sublime impression upon me. It was poetry, but it was not love at all, though people have since wanted to interpret my attachment to her as passion. I loved her until death, without ever thinking that she was a woman. I had seen her as a goddess at Terni! . . .
>
> This charming apparition at Terni was then about eighteen.

Lamartine returned to his English wife and to his post as Embassy Secretary at Florence. Delphine, with her mother, returned to the adulation of Paris. In 1830 Théophile Gautier saw her at the famous first night of *Hernani*. "When she came into her box, and leant forward to look at the audience, which was not the least curious part of the entertainment, her beauty . . . suspended the turmoil for a moment, and earned her a triple round of applause." The vision was so clear in his mind that, forty-two years later, Gautier recalled it again in *L'Histoire du Romantisme*:

> Mademoiselle Gay, . . . who was already famous as a poetess, drew all eyes by her fair beauty. She naturally had the pose and costume that she has in the famous portrait by Hersent: a white dress, a blue sash, long spirals of golden hair, her arm folded and her fingertip touching her cheek in an attitude of admiring attention. That Muse always seemed to be listening to an Apollo. Lamartine and Victor

MADAME DE GIRARDIN

Hugo were her great friends, she worshipped their genius until her final hour, and only when her beautiful white hand turned cold did it let the censer fall. That evening, that ever-memorable evening of *Hernani*, like a simple art student who had gone in before two o'clock with a red ticket, she applauded the shocking beauties, the rebellious touches of genius. . .

Gautier stopped in mid-sentence, for these were the last words he wrote before he died.

Meanwhile, Lamartine recorded that Delphine's dual celebrity as a beauty and a genius:

. . .increased with the seasons. As soon as she appeared in theatres, at fêtes, in academies, a murmur of admiration ran through the crowd, all eyes were turned towards her to gaze at her. Young men extolled her charms, old men lamented that her beauty must be fatal to her happiness. People asked one another anxiously how a woman, used to living on incense in a world that had only been a temple for her, could content herself with a single heart, with an obscure place at a husband's side. . .

People found her too grand for an ordinary husband; they dreamed for her of some or other destiny that was larger than life. They did not know her. She wanted one heart alone; she knew how to adapt herself to the humblest conditions of ordinary life, provided that love, that poetry of the heart, was not absent from her destiny.

Despite her novel-writing, Mme. Gay was far from rich; she and Delphine were obliged to live in a squalid entresol in the rue Gaillon, near the Tuileries. Yet, despite these indifferent surroundings, the most distinguished Parisians continued eagerly to visit them. When Lamartine returned to Paris, he noticed that one young man was often standing behind Delphine's chair. He was a slight young man who hardly seemed past his adolescence.

He spoke little [remembered Lamartine], and he was not named; he seemed to live in a familiar intimacy with the two women, like a brother or a relation who had come back from some distant journey, and naturally resumed his place in the house.

This young man had his eyes on Delphine all the time; he talked to her in a low voice. She would casually turn her noble face to answer him, or smile at him over the back of her chair.

I asked her mother the name of this unknown young man. His strong, fine face inspired involuntary attention and curiosity. Her mother told me that it was M. Emile de Girardin. She told me his history; she consulted me about vague ideas of marriage. I told her

JOANNA RICHARDSON

that the young man had one of those faces that pierced the shadows and mastered fate, and that, in the realm of intelligence, the richest dowry was youth, love and talent.

Soon afterwards I returned to my post abroad; and, while I was abroad, I learned that the charming apparition of the cascade had become Mme. Emile de Girardin.

Girardin had been born on June 21, 1806, the illegitimate son of Comte Alexandre de Girardin, one day to be General, and Grand Veneur to Charles X, and his mistress, Mme. Dupuy. On his falsified birth certificate, he was recorded as Emile Delamothe. He was left with foster parents, and both his father and mother hoped to forget about his existence. As a young man, however, he had discovered the facts about his birth. In 1826, when he was poverty-stricken in Paris, he wrote ·Emile. Part novel and part autobiography, it recorded the trials and struggles of an illegitimate son. In those Romantic days it had an extraordinary success.

Soon afterwards its author boldly took the name Emile de Girardin. It is said that his father not only accepted his paternity, but ensured that Emile was given the post of Inspecteur-Adjoint des Beaux-Arts. The post was unpaid, but it brought its holder some useful social contacts. These led him to the salon of Sophie Gay. On June 1, 1831, he married Delphine. This marriage, wrote Mrs. Challice in 1864, "was a subject of astonishment to many of the bride's admirers; but now as then it were impertinent to speculate upon its causes, or to attempt to unveil her reasons for accepting M. de Girardin as a husband."

Delphine de Girardin was intensely maternal. Once, in 1832, she hoped to have a child; but her hopes were disappointed. George Sand attempted to console her: "You have a mission; had you been a mother, three-quarters of your life would have been lost to that mission. You are a queen of society and an author." Mme. de Girardin replied: "The world has served only to divert me from my solitude." Her unfulfilled wish for a child was the deep disappointment of her life. Often, in her writing, she revealed her unsatisfied love of children. It was a sign of her maternal nature that when her husband presented her with his illegitimate son, Alexandre, she accepted him at once as her own.

Her marriage was not only childless; within a few years, so it seems, it had suffered a crisis. Delphine had never lacked admirers. In the mid-1830s, a Parisian boulevardier, Duranton, fell in love with her and tried to persuade her to elope with him. She refused, as

MADAME DE GIRARDIN

she had refused many other such suggestions. Duranton killed himself. This episode created an unbridgeable gulf between husband and wife. From the time that he suspected her, wrongly, of infidelity, Girardin was "the husband of every wife in Paris except his own."

Late in 1832 the Girardins had settled in the rue Saint-Georges, and Delphine had established her literary salon. Already she showed her benign, delightful influence. For twenty-five years she was the link between all the rivals in talent and in glory who frequented her salon. She prevented Victor Hugo from quarrelling with Lamartine, she encouraged Gautier, she consoled George Sand; for each of them she had the word that charmed; she delighted them by her laughter even when she wished to weep. Men of opposing political parties talked together happily in her presence; men of letters forgot their rivalries. One evening, in front of Balzac, Hugo, Dumas and Alfred de Musset, Delphine and Lamartine both recited their unpublished poems. "Among all these people," said Count Apponyi, the Austrian diplomat, "there was also Mme. Victor Hugo, very ordinary as to her outward appearance, yet still beautiful. She talked a good deal, but with wit, perhaps with a little too much studied elegance. Nonetheless, all these gentlemen seemed to appreciate her very much. Mme. Gay told me that she preferred the husband to the wife. This hardly surprised me. Mme. Gay does not seem to me to be indulgent to women."

Delphine herself was always indulgent; but indulgence was a quality that Girardin did not possess. He was bitter, and he was hard. His illegitimate birth remained a burden to him. It had also given him the incentive to equal, and to surpass, those who were not afflicted with this intolerable stigma. He professed constant scorn, it was said, for literature pure and simple; he chose the newspaper industry as he would have chosen mining if his tastes had led him to metallurgy. In 1836 he founded and edited a brilliant newspaper, *La Presse*. At the fabulously low price of forty francs a year, it allowed him to threaten every rival in journalism. He created the popular press in France.

He was operating at a time when he could commission novels from Dumas, Eugène Sue and Balzac. His list of contributors also included Gautier (as art critic), Victor Hugo (on social questions), George Sand, Lamartine and Gérard de Nerval. If Emile de Girardin was an exacting employer, his wife was the most graceful of presiding deities. It was said that she had advised him to make

JOANNA RICHARDSON

Gautier the literary editor of *La Presse*. But among the contributors was Balzac, far less amenable as a journalist than he had been as host or guest; and Gautier found diplomacy difficult. "My lovely queen," went his note to Mme. de Girardin, "if I'm to go on getting caught between Emile the anvil and Balzac the hammer, I shall resign my office. I'd sooner plant cabbages or rake the paths in your garden." Mme. de Girardin answered, "I have a very satisfactory gardener, thank you. Go on keeping order in the palace."

From the rue Saint-Georges, the Girardins moved to an apartment in the rue Laffitte, which they shared with Dujardin, the joint proprietor of *La Presse*. Gautier recalled Delphine in her new setting.

> The whole apartment was hung with water-green woollen damask. Its glaucous tone, like a nereid's, could only be borne by the complexion of an irreproachable blond. She had not chosen this shade out of malice, but brunettes who strayed into this green cavern looked as yellow as quinces, or as red as furies.
>
> She received her friends in her bedroom . . . It was a very long time before we divined the bed behind the folds of the curtains. There, after the Opéra and the Bouffes, or before the social round began, between eleven o'clock and midnight, there came Lamartine, Victor Hugo, Balzac, Lautour-Mézeray, Eugéne Sue, Alphonse Karr, Cabarrus, Chassériau—not all at once, but certainly some of them every evening. Alfred de Musset also appeared there at long intervals. Mme. Emile de Girardin was extremely proud of her friends: they were her coquetry, her elegance, her luxury. She rightly felt that no festivity with ten thousand candles, a forest of camellias, and the scintillation of all the diamonds of Golconda, was worth those three or four chairs thus occupied round her hearth.

Mme. de Girardin remained a versatile woman of letters. In 1832 she had published *Le Lorgnon*, a fantasy about a man who, thanks to a magic eyeglass, could read through the hypocrisy of words. Perhaps the eyeglass was a symbol of her husband's penetrating mind. Another of her books was to have a personal origin. Balzac had quarrelled with Girardin; and Balzac had written to her, sadly: "Your salon was almost the only one I wanted to go to; I found myself on a friendly footing there. You cannot notice my absence . . ." Mme. de Girardin noticed it, and she was anxious for him to return. As Balzac had an elaborate walking-stick, she wrote *La Canne de Monsieur de Balzac*, the story of a walking-stick that brought both wealth and happiness to its user. On March 16, 1836

MADAME DE GIRARDIN

she sent Balzac an invitation: "This evening I shall be reciting some poetry which will appear in a novel called *La Canne de Monsieur de Balzac*. It would be most shameful if you were not here . . . So mind you come!" Balzac did not come, because the note arrived too late; but, on October 1, Girardin began a letter to him: "My dear sulker . . ." The conversation was resumed, and Balzac was reconquered.

Delphine helped her friends not only as Mme. de Girardin, but as "le Vicomte de Launay." On September 28, 1836, soon after the birth of *La Presse*, she had adopted this pseudonym, and under it published the first of her *Lettres parisiennes*. She was to contribute these dazzling gossip columns until September 3, 1848. The Vicomte de Launay fiercely defended Mme. de Girardin's friends when it was a question of a drama by Dumas, of Hugo's election to the Académie, of George Sand or Balzac. The Vicomte always had a gracious word for Horace Vernet, Liszt and Rossini, and acclaimed the appearance of Rachel on the stage.

"Dear Vicomte," wrote Gautier when he was about to begin a story: "Scribble down the most pretentious possible clothes for Mlle. Féliciana . . . Describe a provincial friend for me, well-to-do and in bad taste." And again: "I beg you, send me a few details about Chopin's concert!" "Chopin's concert," replied the Vicomte, "will be held on Wednesday February 16 in the Salle Pleyel. Would you be kindness itself and say so today in your article, with that grace which belongs to you alone?" Gautier asked Delphine to submit his ideas to Girardin. "I have revealed your plans to *le Patron*," she replied, "and he approves. Can you give him articles *this week?* He asks me to tell you that you must say nothing about the Théâtre Italien. Not a word, that's orders. Nothing good, and nothing bad— just nothing." In 1851, on a visit to the Great Exhibition in London, Gautier found himself short of money. He was—and his hesitation is hardly surprising—too unsure of his reception to ask Emile de Girardin for an advance; and he evaded the request by an invocation to that most human of deities, Girardin's wife:

Madame,
    . . . I have seen Lahore, Calcutta, Kashmir, Benares, Hyderabad under the crystal bell at Hyde Park, and in three hours I became as strong as several Hevas on matters concerning the Ganges. I felt like an elephant among the bamboos and I recognised my native country, for if I appear to have been born in Paris, it is pure illusion; by Brahma, Vishnu and Shiva I swear that I now remember sitting on a white ox with two humps. I am going to write this journey of three thousand

JOANNA RICHARDSON

leagues and three thousand years in three articles which I will send *La Presse* from London because I want to have the things before my eyes—pacify your husband and tell him to send me the money in London so that I can come home, for I have little more than 28 thousand francs on me [sic] and I am beginning to be afraid that I shall have no money as Prince Soltikoff said at Allahabad.

Your *éléphant*-in-ordinary,
THEOPHILE GAUTIER.

It was not the first time that Delphine de Girardin had helped to smooth the path for her *éléphant*, but she responded with engaging promptitude. In her largely illegible hand she dashed off a note to the manager of *La Presse*, asking him to ransom his contributor. The money was dispatched next day (with a warning) to London. Girardin was repaid by three lyrical accounts of the Indian exhibition at the Crystal Palace.

> We hear unceasingly of the intellectual poverty of our salons [reported the Vicomte de Launay], of the incapacity of men of the world, of the futility of their ideas, and littleness of their views; and we hear all these phrases everywhere, even in a salon, seated between Lamartine and Victor Hugo, or between Berryer and Odilon Barrot, who are, in our opinion, as delightful in conversation in French salons, as they are in poetry and oratory for the nation at large.

Mme. de Girardin spoke with asperity; and she spoke with expert understanding. In one of her *Lettres parisiennes* she returned to the subject, and happily discoursed on the art of conversation.

> The fate of conversation depends on three things: the quality of the speakers, the harmony of minds, and the material arrangement of the salon. By material arrangement we mean the complete disarrangement of all the furniture. An entertaining conversation can never begin in a salon where the furniture is symmetrically arranged. . .
>
> The disposition of a salon is like that of an English garden. This apparent disorder is not an effect of chance; on the contrary it is the ultimate art, the result of the most fortunate combinations; there are clumps of chairs and sofas, as there are clumps of trees and shrubs; don't make your salon a parterre, but an English garden. . .
>
> There is another thing that one must remember in order to have an interesting conversation, and that is not to bother about it at all. . . Any premeditation prevents a conversation from being agreeable. You go to see each other; you talk about the good weather and the bad; everyone says, unaffectedly, what passes through his head; some are grave, others extravagant; some are old, and others are young;

MADAME DE GIRARDIN

some are profound, and several are innocent. Madame asks a malicious question; Monsieur makes a biting answer. An enthusiast eagerly tells a story, a *frondeur* makes a harsh criticism; a gossip interrupts the discussion, an epigram wakes it up, a passionate tribute sets it afire . . . A wild joke brings it to an end, and puts everyone into agreement. Time passes, people separate; everyone is happy, everyone has had his say, a happy word that he did not think he was destined to utter. Ideas have circulated; people have learned a story that they did not know, an interesting detail; they are still laughing about someone's mad idea, the charming innocence of that young girl, the witty persistence of that old scholar, and it happens that, without premeditation, and without a plan for conversation, they have talked.

They continued to talk in her salon; and an evening spent in her society was, it was said, the best edition of all her works. In her salon she often chose to talk her *Lettres parisiennes* before she wrote them. The Tenth Muse had been transformed. Before 1831, she could not be anything but an eloquent rhetorician; what she had said about love until then was little but the amplification of some poetic theme. But Mme. de Girardin was now a very distinguished woman, in a very intelligent society, and she did not close her eyes to it or stop up her ears. She could reveal, without embarrassment, the secret of many comedies, or, like the artist she was, be flippant about everything, even about the thoughts and the characters whom she most respected.

Once upon a time [she wrote], women could not spell, but they could dance, and they attracted much attention. Now that they speak English and Italian, and can improvise in French, now that they read British reviews, the histories of M. Mignet, and even the speeches of the Chamber,—now that they can support conversation with the men —the men leave them alone in their glory. Oh, women! women! They cannot understand that their first duty, their first interest, is to be attractive. Men do not seek them to share their cares, but to dispel them. Knowledge, for women, is a luxury; the necessity is grace, elegance, and the power of pleasing.

Besides being a sparkling novelist and journalist, Mme. de Girardin was also a dramatist. On December 6, 1841 sixty people gathered in her salon, among them the Ministers of Justice and Public Instruction, Lamartine (who had come specially from Saint-Point), Victor Hugo and his wife, and Balzac. Mme. de Girardin, wearing a black velvet dress, took her place on a platform between Balzac and Hugo, and began to read her play. After the second act,

JOANNA RICHARDSON

Hugo stood up, with his hand on his heart, and announced: "It is superb!"

Delphine was to write more than one play for Rachel. The great actress was sometimes Girardin's mistress; and she remained his wife's devoted friend. She was largely responsible for making Delphine write *Cléopâtre*, which was triumphantly performed on November 13, 1847. Some time later, Rachel wrote to the dramatist:

> Very dear Madame,
> How kind you would be if you agreed to come and dine with me today, with the nice Alexandre. I already have permission from your noble husband. You will find no one here except people who adore you. . . My carriage will be at your door at six precisely.
> Your faithful
LADY RACHEL.

In 1843 the Girardins had moved from the rue Laffitte to the rue de Chaillot, off the Champs-Elysées. This little villa, in the style of a Greek temple, had been built during the Empire, and Mirecourt, the prolific writer of popular biographies, recorded that

> Emile—an intrepid speculator—had bought the villa very cheaply. At first he said that he was buying it simply to resell it. For twelve years, Mme. de Girardin therefore had a temporary home. She lived on the first floor. As for her husband, he shut himself up on the second, in a kind of rotunda, where only Jean, an old servant, more devoted to Monsieur than to Madame, was allowed to enter and to let in visitors.
> The two reception rooms were on the ground floor. Again, as a temporary measure, they had been furnished with mean furniture, and the hangings were chintz; but the absence of luxury did not prevent the most select society and people of the highest distinction from meeting there. . .
> Mme. de Girardin's *cercle* was open every evening, and every evening it was filled by the most remarkable celebrities in Paris. M. de Girardin hardly made an appearance, and no-one asked for him.

Delphine herself rarely passed beyond the threshold. She was only to be found beneath her own roof. Gautier came to visit her in the rue de Chaillot. "It was in the small drawing-room that Mme. Emile de Girardin always sat; she used to work there, half-enclosed by a great Chinese screen, on which, on a black background, curious birds were fluttering through bamboos and exotic plants.

MADAME DE GIRARDIN

She was easily distracted by the pleasure of some friendly visit; at home she always wore a very ample peignoir with no belt. . ."

In the late 1840s, observed another visitor, "one found her almost always alone, the pen in her hand . . . Those who saw her in these latter days were struck with the solemn, majestic and serene air which her more mature beauty had assumed. She wept for children which she had never had. She would have been a fine mother for a son; the predominant trait in her character was heroism."

On February 25, 1854, her new play, *La Joie fait peur*, was performed at the Théâtre-Français. On December 16, at the Gymnase, there followed *Le Châpeau d'un horloger*. She was thinking of new works when, in 1855, she was halted in mid-career. She suffered from cancer of the stomach.

Lamartine came to see her in the rue de Chaillot:

> The last time, I was shown into a little low room on the ground floor. She had taken refuge there to avoid the noise of the workmen, who were redecorating her apartments. . .
>
> Despite the cold weather, a big glass door was open on to a little courtyard which was enclosed by high walls on every side. In the middle of this little courtyard, a marble fountain shed a melancholy trickle of tinkling water. . .
>
> I found her scarcely changed. . . The conversation was smiling, light, affectionate, as befitted an invalid who was coming back to life. . .
>
> We were stupefied to learn, next day, that she had died.

Delphine de Girardin died on June 29, 1855. She was fifty-one. She was buried on July 2, at the Cimetière Montmartre—where, in 1881, her husband was to be buried beside her. "Those who had known her only by name wept for her; those who had loved her," wrote Lamartine, "will never be consoled." Méry, the Marseillais man of letters, passed the rue de Chaillot and lamented that death had blown out the lamps that had been lit the previous evening, that "all was extinguished, everything had vanished." Hugo, in his exile, had written the best epitaph. "When I think of France, and I always do," he had told her, "I think of you. I feel that you are part of its image."

JOANNA RICHARDSON

SELECTED BIBLIOGRAPHY

Challice, Mrs. A.E.. ed. *French Authors at Home.* 2 vols. (Booth, 1864).

[Girardin, Mme. Emile de] *Le Vicomte de Launay. Lettres Parisiennes par Mme. Emile de Girardin.* Précédeés d'une introduction par Théophile Gautier. 4 vols. (Michel Lévy, 1857).

_____ *Esprit de Mme. de Girardin.* Avec préface par M. de Lamartine. (Hetzel, 1862).

Malo, Henri. *La Gloire du Vicomte de Launay. Delphine Gay de Girardin.* (Emile Paul, 1925).

Mirecourt, Eugène de. *Mme de Girardin.* (Librairie des Contemporains, 1870).

Reclus, Maurice. *Emile de Girardin. Le Créateur de la Presse Moderne.* (Hachette, 1934).

Richardson, Joanna. *Théophile Gautier: His Life and Times* (Reinhardt, 1958).

Saint-Amand, Imbert de. *Mme de Girardin.* (Plon, 1875).

Séché, Léon. *Muses romantiques. Delphine Gay, Mme de Girardin.* (Mercure de France, 1910).

Willard, L. tr. *Celebrated Saloons,* by Madame Gay; and *Parisian Letters,* by Madame de Girardin. Translated from the French by L. Williard. (Boston, Mass., Wm. Crosby and H.P. Nichols, 1851).

MADAME DE LIEVEN

A Russian in Paris

Peter Quennell

During the early autumn of 1835, an important Russian visitor arrived in Paris, the celebrated Princess de Lieven, whose husband, now the governor of the Tsarevich, the future Alexander II, had been the Russian Ambassador to the Court of St. James's from 1812 to 1834. After those happy years, when she had exercised more influence, was said to have known more secrets than most contemporary British politicians, and became one of the brightest luminaries of the London social world, she found St. Petersburg and the etiquette of the Russian court under Nicholas I intolerably tedious. A private tragedy, the death of her two youngest sons, killed in the same month by the same illness, had increased her longing to escape. The Emperor gave his permission, merely stipulating that her place of residence should not be France; and her husband, a devoted courtier, urged she should obey their sovereign. She disregarded them both, and, having reached Paris, defiantly settled down, first at the Hotel de la Terrasse, rue de Rivoli, then at the corner of the neighbouring rue Saint-Florentin, to begin a new and independent life.

Dorothea de Lieven, christened Dorothea von Benckendorff, the offspring of an ancient Livonian family, was born in 1785. Her mother, companion to the Empress Maria, wife of the demented Paul I, had died when she was only twelve. The Empress, a kindly woman, had supervised her upbringing and married her off, at the age of fifteen, to Count Christopher Lieven, a distinguished young soldier, whom the Emperor Paul appointed his Minister of War, and whom his successor, Alexander I, rewarded with the London Embassy. There the Mme. de Lieven discovered her true gifts. Her husband was an industrious and dutiful, but not a very clever man, nick-named *"Vraiment?"* by his English acquaintances, owing to his expression of mild surprise and polite incredulity on hearing any piece of news. Madame de Lieven, however, soon contrived to establish a secondary diplomatic service; and during the 1820s, over the heads of their accredited ambassadors, she dispatched regular reports to the Emperor of Russia and the Austrian Chancellor Prince Metternich. The knowledge she imparted was derived from her personal friendships. She made friends easily; and the intimates she chose very often fell in love with her. George IV, after his accession to the throne in 1820, paid the Ambassadress effusive homage. She was always welcome at the Cottage, near Windsor Castle, and at the King's seaside folly, the Brighton Pavilion, where he entertained his elderly mistress, Lady Conyngham, and her brood of grown-up children. At the Pavilion, the atmosphere, she discovered, was so luxurious as to be exhausting and oppressive. "I do not believe that, since the days of Heliogabalus, there have been such magnificence and such luxury . . . One spends the evening half-lying on cushions; the lights are dazzling; there are perfumes, music, liqueurs . . ."[1] "Devil take me," the Duke of Wellington remarked, "I think I must have got into bad company," when he arrived for dinner and looked around him at the scene.

Madame de Lieven valued the King's friendship and the political insights it afforded her, but also appreciated his absurdity. Although deeply enamoured of Lady Conyngham, he was an inveterate philanderer:

The King and I amuse ourselves (she told Metternich, on June 14, 1826) and he tries to play little tricks on me. He persists in his advances . . . The other day . . . after luncheon, we had all gone to get ready to go out. My suite looks . . . on to a very dark tree-shaded walk . . . All the windows reach to the ground . . . while I was in front of the glass, the King slipped quietly behind the hornbeam at the end of the walk. I opened the window, and asked him if he were waiting for me. He put his finger to his lips and, with gestures and passionate glances, begged to be allowed to come in . . . It was so rude to laugh that I restrained myself; but I turned away, called my maid, and asked her for my hat. When the King saw her coming, he took fright . . . and fled so

PETER QUENNELL

hurriedly that he nearly fell; with the result that I had time to go back quickly to the drawing-room . . . when he saw me, he made me a deep bow in the style of Louis XIV.

From this passage it is clear that Madame de Lieven had not only a keen sense of humour but considerable descriptive gifts— qualities that sparkle again and again through the letters her favourite correspondent, Prince Metternich, received. She had first encountered him, and briefly become his mistress, during the autumn of 1818 at the Congress of Aix-la-Chapelle, where Allied diplomatists gathered to debate the evacuation of French territory; and the Austrian Chancellor, known by his antagonists as the "Grand Inquisitor of Europe", an arch-reactionary and defender of absolute rule, whom every liberal feared and hated, had quickly noticed her attractions. Metternich was then forty-five, magnificently handsome in his bland Olympian way and a famous *homme-à-succès*. With Madame de Lieven he rapidly succeeded. He had not forgotten, he wrote a month later, the details of their earliest meeting:

> The hour I spent sitting at your feet showed me it was a place I liked to be. When I returned home, I felt that I had known you for many years. . . On the 29th, I did not see you. On the 30th, I felt that the previous day had been singularly cold and devoid of meaning. I forgot just when it was you came to my box in the theatre. *You* were feverish—*mon amie*, you belonged to me![2]

Metternich's letters to Madame de Lieven are far less agreeable reading than her long replies. A conceited, profoundly self-satisfied lover, he abounds in philosophic generalizations and dramatic airs and graces, and gravely congratulates his mistress on her treatment of her unsuspecting husband: "You know that I wish you to be good, gentle and excellent in your behaviour towards him. I do not have his rights; and those I have myself he cannot share . . . I have never disturbed a marriage; I respect *the law* . . ." After the memorable autumn of 1818, they were seldom in the same city, and could only meet if a conference mustered the European diplomatic corps. Letter-writing was now their substitute for love. "My letters," she told him in 1826, the closing year of their relationship, "have been a most faithful record of everything that came to my knowledge. . . ." And later, on November 22, answering his hundred-and-seventy-fourth epistle: "You ought to write to me more often . . . we would be hard put to it, you and I, to find in the whole world people of our own calibre. Our hearts are well matched, our minds too . . . you will find no-one better than me. If you meet your like, show him to me. Goodbye."

That was the last letter she wrote Metternich, the last, at all events, that she preserved. In 1827 he contracted a second marriage—with Marie-Antoinette von Leykam, who, although young and beautiful, was the daughter of comparatively un-distinguished parents. The relationship was thereupon broken off; and, through the good offices of the Duke of Wellington (whose help was constantly invoked at a time of crisis, whether it were political or personal) each sent back the other's letters; from her own, she copied out the passages that she thought particularly informative.

Meanwhile, she was beginning to despise Metternich. She had come to believe, she remarked, that some usurper must have appropriated the Prince's name, and that this pseudo-statesman was responsible for the many egregious blunders he had recently committed. Madame de Lieven often changed her opinions. *"Pour elle,"* observed a contemporary diarist, *"tout se réduisait à des questions de personnes"*; and it is true that her private feelings exerted a strong effect on her political allegiances. During the early days of her liaison with Metternich, she had acted as a diplomatic link between the European *ultras*; and, as an arch-conservative, she had gained the friendship of two great British Tories, Castlereagh and Wellington, and, among the King's familiars at the Cottage and the Pavilion, had joined a secret conspiracy to "blow up Mr. Canning", the chief representative of Liberal views. Yet, little by little, Canning's energy and eloquence had captured her imagination; and Canning was presently succeeded by the urbane and dignified Lord Grey, enlightened author of the first Reform Bill.

Madame de Lieven, she frankly confessed, was "a woman, and very much a woman". Though scarcely beautiful—in London the same friends who had nick-named her husband *"Vraiment?"* had also labelled her "The Snipe", in reference to her long neck and distinctive beak-like nose—she possessed, and frequently exer-cised, a high degree of magnetic feminine charm, which Lawrence caught when he painted the beguiling portrait that now hangs in the Tate Gallery. She was elegant, too; her clothes were always admired; and, at one moment, when she briefly revisited Russia,

Ralph Sneyd, a gadabout man of letters, published a melodious valediction:

> She has gone, as the *Herald* announces,
> To latitudes wilder and colder;
> She has gone with her pearls and her flounces,
> She had gone with the bows on her shoulder.

To these qualities, and to her knowledge of the European *grand monde*, she owed the position that she held in London. No other foreign Ambassadress had been more readily accepted; and, as a Patroness of Almack's, the fashionable dancing club, to which only half-a-dozen officers of the Foot Guards had received tickets of admission, together with her fellow patronesses, the Ladies Jersey, Castlereagh, Sefton and Cowper, she ruled the English aristocratic world and pronounced draconian edicts that even the Duke of Wellington could not safely disobey. Her snobism was so natural and so deep-rooted that it became entirely unselfconscious. Thus, a gentleman of middle-class origins who agreed at her well-wishers' request to accompany her across Europe and protect her on the journey, was politely thanked upon arrival for all the trouble he had taken but was told that, since he and she belonged to different social spheres and, no doubt, since they had very different friends, she must bid him goodbye. Another parvenu, whom she had temporarily encouraged, but about whose antecedents, she afterwards discovered, she had been somewhat misinformed, was expelled from her salon, where he had ventured to make his bow, with a single icy remark, *"Monsieur, je ne vous connais pas!"*

Her chief weakness, however, was her haunting dread of boredom; and, in September 1833, Thomas Creevey recorded a conversation he had lately overheard between Madame de Lieven and the Duchesse de Dino, Talleyrand's beloved niece:

> The Lieven's creed was that she *would not* be bored, and the Dino's that she *could not*. The Russian avowed that the instant a person began to bore her, she got up and left him, and nothing could or should extort any civility from her . . . Then the modest Lieven said, "She knew in return she must bore people herself, for she had observed that at dinners she was the only person who had ever an empty chair next to her . . ." "But," said the Dino, "that is from the fear lest they should bore *you*."

Even of her admirers she finally grew tired. Canning had died in 1827; Grey began to lose his fascination. With London, however, and the life she lived there, she was never really bored; and the serious diplomatic dispute that took place in 1833 over the appointment of a new British ambassador at St. Petersburg—Lord Palmerston, the Foreign Secretary, had proposed Sir Stratford Canning, whom the Russian government considered an impossible choice—caused her so much alarm that she set off for Russia alone, hoping to allay the crisis. She had a warm welcome; the Emperor came to meet her, carried her to the Palace in his carriage, and straight into his consort's dressing-room; and she returned home somewhat reassured. But Palmerston, although she asserted that he owed his present position largely to her influence with Lord Grey, and that she had brought him a personal message from Nesselrode, the Russian Chancellor, obstinately refused to budge; and Grey—"an old woman!" Madame de Lieven exclaimed— supported his outrageous Foreign Secretary. She could do no more. On August 30, 1834, M. de Lieven received his recall, but was also informed that he had been honoured with the post of governor to the Heir Apparent. At this news, remembered Madame de Lieven, "my husband raised his hands in joy, and I lifted mine in sorrow".

Once she had regained St. Petersburg, where the Lievens learned that they were to occupy an apartment under the same roof as the imperial household, she faced the situation bravely; and, having already assisted M. de Lieven by seconding his am- bassadorial efforts, she now herself undertook the problem of educating the sixteen-year-old Heir, "the most delicious young man she had ever encountered", though he needed worldly polish. But, after the London embassy, Tsarkoe-Selo seemed dull, the discipline of Russian court-life oppressive, and the Russian climate in- sufferably harsh. During early March 1835, she heard that her two beloved sons had died. To remain in Russia was thenceforward out of the question; and, her doctors having warned her against Italy, her husband escorted her as far as Berlin. Since she felt that she should not revisit London—it contained too many memories— Paris seemed the obvious refuge; and in mid-September, accom- panied by her niece Marie, daughter of her brother Constantine, she finally arrived there. The Emperor was unlikely to forgive her, she said. Almost more hurtful, the patient M. de Lieven, furious that

PETER QUENNELL

his master should be disobeyed, threatened to cut off her allowance.

In 1835, Louis-Philippe [son of Philippe-Egalité] crowned Orléanist *Roi des Français* five years earlier on the fall of Charles X, the Bourbon *Roi de France*, occupied a difficult position between Right and Left. Though he had inherited libertarian beliefs, and sometimes wished to be thought of as *"le roi des barricades"*, the ministers who led his government grew more and more conservative. Such a state of affairs was bound to interest a politically minded woman; but for a while, Madame de Lieven, being much preoccupied with her own sorrows and domestic problems, seems to have avoided public life; and, from Vienna, Metternich expressed surprise that he had as yet heard nothing of her operations. "She must be active one way or another," he said, "for it is not in her character to remain completely quiet." Metternich's suspicions were well founded; by the beginning of the year 1837 she had already achieved a grand political renaissance.

In January the diarist Charles Greville wrote that she appeared to have made for herself an extremely enviable situation. She was at home every evening; and her salon was neutral ground on which the different parties met, so much so that one saw the bitterest adversaries there, engaged in courteous discussion. Among the men of the day she favoured were Molé, an amiable and intelligent man, and, if not the most brilliant of the assemblage, the most sensible and the surest judge; Thiers, by far the most outstanding, replete with wit and conversational verve; and Guizot and Berryer, both full of merit. As their hostess, Madame de Lieven evidently enjoyed herself; but, perhaps to tease her guests, she pretended to disdain the French character, and applaud the moral superiority of England.

The British Ambassadress, Lady Granville (daughter of Georgiana Duchess of Devonshire) was a very old friend; and, in January 1837, she wrote to her sister Lady Carlisle:

> Mme. de Lieven [is] in great beauty and high spirits. She has always an *entourage*; she can keep off bores, because she has the courage to *écraser* them. The sublimities sometimes clash, but that for her taste is a small evil. It would kill me to have Berryer and Molé . . . looking daggers at each other, *mais elle sait nager* and gets out of every difficulty. The pleasantest women here, in my opinion, go constantly

to her, Mmes. Appony, Schönburg, Durazzo, and Marie, who makes
tea like a Goddess.

That August, Lady Granville wrote Lady Carlisle a second letter:
"Mme. de Lieven is more interesting, amusing and agreeable than I
can say. All she pours forth of all those I am fond of or curious about
makes Paris alive in this dead season." But, fond though she was of
her old friend, she recognized her native arrogance, and, in
September 1838, was delighted to be able to quote, for Lady
Carlisle's benefit, Madame de Lieven's own story of how the no less
imperious Lady Holland had adroitly put her down:

> Ma chère, I was with her. Mme. Durazzo, Molé and Humbolt were
> there. Pasquier[3] was announced. She seemed immensely charmed
> and flattered. "Stay, I beg you," she said to me, "talk to the
> Chancellor." I demur; she implores me not to leave her. I give in; and
> no sooner had I settled down again among the company who are
> watching us than she let her bag drop. She taps me on the shoulder:
> "Pick it up, my dear; pick it up"—and there was I, toute étonnée en
> bonne bête, plunging down on to the carpet to collect her odds and
> ends. Is not this a true and incomparable Holly-ism, taking out of
> Lieven's mouth the taste of the little flutter at the visits and besoin of
> her support, by showing off, what I believe never was seen before,
> Mme. de Lieven as a humble companion?

Madame de Lieven's surprising mildness may have been partly
due to the fact that, during the summer of 1836, a great emotional
discovery had transformed her whole existence. On June 15, 1836,
at dinner with the Duc de Broglie, she had sat next to the solemn
statesman Francois Guizot, and had found him sympathetic. Then,
on June 24, 1837, they had once again met, at Madame de Boigne's[4]
country-house, and had walked together through the park, and
shared melancholy recollections. Each of them had suffered cruel
losses; both, of course, had read Byron's verses and belonged to
the Romantic Age. Madame de Lieven told of her sons' death;
Guizot, too, had recently lost a son and his devoted second wife;
while Madame de Lieven's thirty-eight-year-old marriage had now
become a bitter memory. On that occasion, or during the next few
days, Guizot had spoken the words that, he afterwards assured
her, had irrevocably united them. She had talked of her harrowing
sense of solitude. "You will no longer be alone," he said.

He kept his promise. Until the moment of her death he remained
her lover and companion. Nor was their relationship merely the

PETER QUENNELL

platonic alliance of two disillusioned world-travellers. In 1837 Guizot was fifty, his mistress fifty-three, and perhaps not unlike the time-worn, austerely dignified woman painted by Watts in 1856. Cynical contemporaries sometimes speculated about the nature of their union; but Mérimée declared that, one evening, when, except for M. Guizot, he was Madame de Lieven's last guest—having bidden her a ceremonious farewell, he discovered that he had left his hat behind, and returned unexpectedly to see that the great man had "already taken off his *cordon bleu*". Whether or not their liaison was physical, there seems no doubt that it had a deeply emotional origin, and brought them a degree of calm and contentment they had never felt before.

Possibly because she needed to assess her feelings, Madame de Lieven left Paris towards the end of June, and paid a triumphant visit to London. Her friends, headed by the Duchess of Sutherland, Mistress of the Robes at the court of the new sovereign, welcomed her with open arms; and she was duly presented to the young Victoria, on whom she composed a highly favourable report:

> We were alone for half an hour. There is much reserve and propriety in her conversation, and a touch of timidity that she knows how to combine with a touch of haughtiness. A charming face, open, intelligent, a nicely shaped nose and kiss-worthy cheeks . . . When her ministers leave her, she sings; she is always singing, at her toilette, while her royal robes are put on . . . She wishes to have music after dinner. One runs at break-neck speed . . . All the world is gay with gaiety, young with her youth . . . It is long since anybody so young has occupied the English throne.

During this visit, which lasted until August 1, she wrote Guizot a score of lengthy letters; and Guizot replied at equal length, addressing her first as "Dearest Princess" (in English) and, latterly, as "Dearest" or "Ever Dearest". If his letters were delayed, she plunged into deep despair: "I devour the newspapers. I tremble lest I should read your name connected with some accident." And later: "You cannot have abandoned me! I asked you one day whether you came from heaven or hell. There is something supernatural in the power you exercise! . . . My soul is yours . . . If this letter reaches you, will you not be alarmed by the vivacity, the violence of my sufferings? Can you forgive me for loving so much? I did not know myself, Monsieur, that I was capable of it . . ." Once they were reunited, Guizot calmed her fears: "There is none of your sentiments," he assured her, "that I do not understand, and that does not please me, in the most intimate and most serious sense of the word . . . Keep them all, dearest; they are true notes; harmony will return . . . I am sure that, if you could recover your health, you would no longer be vexed by the troubles of which you complain. You have such a good judgement, such a proud and delicate spirit, that, did the state of your nerves not stand in your way, you would see things and people as they really are. . ."

The happy union of these two very different characters astonished Parisian society. How could the woman Prince Metternich had once loved now consent to become the Egeria, probably the mistress, of plain M. François Guizot? For Guizot's origins were typically middle-class. Born at Nîmes in 1787, the son of a young lawyer guillotined during the Revolution, Guizot, after finishing his education at the University of Geneva, in 1805, reached Paris where he earned his living as a journalist. Then, in 1812, aged twenty-five, he was elected to the Chair of History at the Sorbonne, and, in 1814, appointed Secretary General at the Ministry of the Interior. Guizot now headed the *Doctrinaires*, the moderate Royalists who endeavoured to hold a balance between democracy and the *ancien régime*. He had described his youthful self as "very obscure, very proud, very susceptible and very tender"; but he had also a tremendous fund of nervous energy and a strong determination to succeed. He possessed an excellent mind; and the interests that absorbed him were both political and academic. From 1820 onwards he devoted much of his attention to the study of European history; and his *Histoire de la révolution d'Angleterre*, a highly original work, appeared in 1827.

Having opposed the reactionary policies of Charles X, in 1830 he joined Louis-Philippe's first cabinet as Minister of the Interior, and in 1832 became Minister of Public Instruction, retaining cabinet rank until 1836, when, under Thiers's new government, he was temporarily set aside. The middle-aged man, who conquered Madame de Lieven's heart, was at once a distinguished political figure and an eminent historian. But he did not invariably please. Many of his contemporaries voted him cold and severe; towards the end of his life, he acquired a *"morose renom"*, a forbidding reputation. Beneath his frigid mannerisms, however, still lurked, as his correspondence with Madame de Lieven shows, a passionate and deeply sensitive spirit. He had always needed a feminine confidante; and to both his wives, the first fourteen years his senior,

PETER QUENNELL

the second seventeen years his junior, and to the children they bore him[5], he had been tenderly devoted. Like Metternich, Guizot was a handsome man, though in a very different and far more scholastic style. His forehead was lofty; his features were clearly cut; he had an arched nose and keen expressive eyes.

Such was the dominant personage for whom Madame de Lieven chose to re-arrange her life, and around whom she organized her salon. From the rue de Rivoli she had moved to the rue Saint-Florentin, taking over the entresol of the house that had once been Talleyrand's. There she received all that she found most interesting in the worlds of politics and fashion, and established a meeting-place where political opponents agreed temporarily to lay aside their arms. Among her chief guests listed by Charles Greville were Comte Molé, Prime Minister from 1836-1839; Thiers, Guizot's main adversary, Prime Minister from 1834 to 1836, a "perpetual source of fireworks" and author of *Histoire de la révolution* and *Histoire du Consulat et de l'Empire*; and Berryer, the celebrated advocate who would bitterly oppose Napoleon III. Each was a man of formidable intelligence and a well-known conversationalist. The hostess herself, wrote Greville after her death, had had "abilities of a very fine order" and "great tact and finesse . . . Nothing could exceed the charm of her conversation, or her grace, ease, and tact in society . . . Though taking an ardent pleasure in agreeableness, and peculiarly susceptible of being bored, she was . . . full of politeness and good breeding, and possessed the faculty of turning every one to account . . ."

Conversation at the rue Saint-Florentin was, of course, primarily political; but the Duchesse Décazes, a somewhat hostile critic, records that she once heard Madame de Lieven discuss amusingly, and in very great detail, the superiority of the old-fashioned hooped skirt over the modern petticoat. Her manner of speech, said an English acquaintance, Sir Sidney Ralph, whatever her subject might be, had brevity and an epigrammatic precision, devoid of affected phrases, and was at once easy and gracious, lively, sometimes flippant, but always perfectly to the point. As in the past, besides encouraging and entertaining her guests, she also made good use of them; and it was believed that she passed on political news not only to her friends at the French Court but to the Emperor Nicholas at St. Petersburg. Since her husband had died, still unreconciled with her, in 1838, she had regained the Emperor's favour, and now wrote regular dispatches to his consort, which were immediately read aloud over the imperial breakfast table.

Guizot's political position, while he held office, was said to have been based on "an inherited conservatism tempered by a certain degree of acquired scepticism"; and, during his last premiership, which lasted from 1840 until 1848, his conservative tendencies became more and more pronounced. As Louis-Philippe, who was caricatured by Daumier as *la Poire*—the homely fruit that his head was thought to resemble—grew increasingly unpopular, Guizot, too, aroused a storm of hatred. In February 1848, the government prohibited a "Reform banquet" arranged by the Liberal opposition; on the twenty-second rioting broke out, and the National Guard, with loud shouts of " *A bas Guizot!*" and "*Vive la réforme!*" marched along the rue de Rivoli. Madame de Lieven, earlier that year, had been suffering from boredom, the state of mind she most dreaded, and had told the Duchesse de Dino that she needed "*quelque grande dislocation, bouleversement, complication*" to restore her natural spirits. Her wish was soon granted; and, early on the twenty-third, having sewn her jewels and some ready money into her dress, she made a swift and secret exit. A fortnight later, disguised as the wife of an English artist, she successfully set sail for England.

Guizot had preceded her; they were happily reunited. But the boredom that had threatened her at the rue Saint-Florentin presently swept down again; and that autumn she accompanied Guizot to Brighton, the scene of so many past adventures. There, after twenty-six years, she came face to face with Metternich, himself an exile from Vienna, and met his amiable third wife. She was profoundly disillusioned. Her Olympian seducer, now seventy-five years old, had lost both elegance and dignity:

> I see M. and Mme. de Metternich every day (she wrote to a friend in Paris). She, stout, vulgar, natural, good and easy to get on with. He, full of serenity and self-satisfaction, interminably loquacious, very long-winded, very slow, very heavy, very metaphysical, boring when he talks of himself and his own infallibility, charming when he speaks of the past and, above all, of the Emperor Napoleon.

Once the storm of revolution had safely passed, Guizot and Madame de Lieven returned to Paris and the salon re-opened. For a while, Charles Greville noted, Madame de Lieven appeared ready to support the Bourbon cause and even tentatively waved the

PETER QUENNELL

Legitimists' white flag; but, before long, her interest shifted towards the future Napoleon III. The coup d'état of December 1851 was the kind of *bouleversement* that she had always found inspiriting; and, although other salons prudently closed their doors, she continued to receive. Soon she was fascinated by the appearance of a new star, the beautiful Spanish girl, Eugénie de Montijo, who in 1853 would marry the Emperor of the French. During her sad old age at Farnborough, the Empress described how, before her engagement had been publicly announced, the Duc de Morny, Napoleon's half-brother and chief adviser, had insisted that she should visit the *doyenne* of the salons, and she had met and received the graceful attentions of a"*grande vieille femme, maigre, sèche et dure*".

Among those who observed the scene was the Duc de Broglie; and he has left a vivid description, almost Proustian in its satirical acumen, of the hostess's behaviour. Mlle. de Montijo's prospects at the time were still uncertain; but, "when I beheld the mistress of the house place herself on a low chair beside the sofa where she had placed the young beauty, I understood that the choice had been made, and that it was high time to offer my homages unless I wished to be lost in the throng of expectant courtiers . . ." Evidently Madame de Lieven saw brilliant days ahead; and she was deeply shocked by the outbreak of the Crimean War, which, as she was still a Russian subject, obliged her to abandon Paris. She vegetated in Brussels, fretful and aggrieved, until 1856. But then, wrote the Comte de Sainte-Aulaire, "her salon regained its diplomatic importance"; and, if it was no longer crowded, she could count on sufficient guests to dispel the hideous pangs of boredom.

She was now seventy-three, an old and tired woman; and by the close of 1856 it seemed clear that she had not very long to live. In January 1857, bronchitis was followed by pneumonia; and, during the night of January 27, Madame de Lieven died. After she had breathed her last, her son Paul, the only member of her family present, handed Guizot a pencil-written letter: "Thank you for twenty years of affection and happiness. Do not forget me. Adieu, adieu . . ." There can be no doubt of her lasting devotion to Guizot. Yet she had never married him; and her reasons she had already explained many years earlier, while she and the Countess Nesselrode were driving in her carriage through the Bois. Some of their friends believed, Madame Nesselrode said, that she might become the statesman's wife. Had the story any basis? "*Ma chere,*

MADAME DE LIEVEN

can you imagine me being announced as Madame Guizot!" she cried, and threw herself laughing back against the cushions.

NOTES

1. She wrote on January 26, 1822. See *The Private Letters of Princess Lieven to Prince Metternich, 1820-1826.* Edited by Peter Quennell, 1937.
2. *Lettres du Prince de Metternich à la Comtesse de Lieven.* Edited by Jean Hanoteau, Paris, 1909.
3. Etienne Denis de Pasquier, 1757-1862; Prefect of Police under Napoleon I; created a Peer of France, 1821; appointed Chancellor of France by Louis Philippe, 1837.
4. Mme. de Boigne occupied the same position in Pasquier's life as did Madame de Lieven in Guizot's.
5. Guillaume Guizot, the son of his second wife, became the close friend of Flaubert, Baudelaire and Renan.

PETER QUENNELL

SPERANZA

A Leaning Tower of Courage

Victoria Glendinning

The room was poorly furnished, the tea was badly served; even in the dim light of a few flickering candles the dust and dinginess was apparent. But the lady of the house was in her element; it was Saturday afternoon, and she was holding her salon. "What mattered the old-fashioned brocade gown, the long gold earrings, or the yellow fichu crossed on her breast and fastened with innumerable enormous brooches, the huge bracelets of turquoise and gold, and the rings on every finger? Her faded splendour was more striking than the most fashionable attire, for she wore that ancient finery with a grace and dignity that robbed it of its grotesqueness."[1] This is Speranza; this is Oscar Wilde's mother.

She was born Jane Francesca Elgee, somewhat earlier than 1826, which was the year she admitted to. She had invented a theory that "Elgee" was a corruption of "Alighieri," thus claiming a descent from Dante; in fact, her great-grandfather Charles Elgee was a bricklayer from County Durham who settled in Dundalk, County Louth, in the 1730s.[2] His son, the most respectable member of the family on her father's side, became Archdeacon of Leighlin. Her mother, Sara Kingsbury, was from a Dublin family well established in the professions of law and medicine. Her mother's sister Henriette married the Rev. Charles Maturin, author of *Melmoth the Wanderer*. When Oscar Wilde in exile called himself Sebastian Melmoth, he took the name from his great-uncle's book.

Jane Francesca's father was an attorney of no distinction; she was probably born in Dublin, though there is no official record of her birth; there is even a slight possibility that she was illegitimate. She was a clever child, a gifted linguist, who had acquired a knowledge of Latin, Greek, French, German and Italian. She matured into a tall, dark, statuesque young woman with fine eyes and an unorthodox interest in politics and history.

In 1851 she married William Robert Wills Wilde; he was thirty-six, she something over twenty-five. She was not his first choice. He loved the actress Helen Faucit; but she married Sir Theodore Martin, biographer of the Prince Consort; and, three months after that wedding, Willie Wilde led Jane Francesca to the altar. It was not a glamourous match for her; Wilde was an educated and scholarly person, a successful Dublin specialist in diseases of the ear and eye; but he was most unprepossessing, uncouth, unkempt, undersized, with a shambling, simian appearance. Nor were his morals of the purest. Women found this ugly little man attractive. Before he married he had already fathered two, and possibly more, families of illegitimate children.

He was an unconventional man; in marrying Jane Francesca he was taking an unconventional wife. She was already notorious for the poems and articles she published under the name "Speranza". In 1842 a nationalist newspaper, *The Nation*, was launched in Dublin; its editor was Charles Gavan Duffy. By the mid-1840s, when famine was already causing desolation and unrest, Speranza was regularly contributing passionately patriotic and anti-British poems and articles; Gavan Duffy called the verses of this ardent female supporter of the Young Ireland movement "virile and sonorous". British officialdom in Ireland, alarmed by the inflammatory influence of *The Nation*, raided the paper's offices and took away material that included a 6,000-word piece, *"Jacta Alea Est"*, written by Speranza and intended as a leading article. The editor was arrested on a charge of treason-felony. Speranza's article, a frank incitement to armed rebellion against the British, was read out in court; she made an impassioned intervention, claiming sole responsibility for the article, and became, briefly, a nationalist heroine.

After her marriage, Speranza continued to write and publish; but, as wife, mother and society hostess, she dropped her demands for armed revolt. When in 1864 Wilde was knighted (for his services to statistical science in connection with the Irish census), she was delighted to become Lady Wilde. Sir William was also appointed Surgeon Oculist in Ordinary to Queen Victoria—had the Queen

VICTORIA GLENDINNING

lost her spectacles while visiting Ireland, for example, Wilde would have been called in. Speranza had her portrait painted, went to the Lord Lieutenant's parties, became happily snobbish. In letters to her son, Oscar Wilde, she always referred to her husband as "Sir William".

The Wildes entertained with enthusiasm, and kept open house at No. 1 Merrion Square, a fine large corner-house which Speranza filled with heavy mahogany, huge oil paintings and Turkish carpets. Bills, duns and even writs overshadowed this splendour; Sir William had, after all, unusually heavy domestic commitments, and spent all his wife's money as well as his own. They were a raffish pair. They had three children: Willie, born in 1852; Oscar, born in 1854; and a daughter, Isola, born in 1859, but who died less than ten years later.

It was on Saturday afternoons that Speranza held her salons at Merrion Square. Anyone and everyone came; Speranza was not fussy. Professor Mahaffy, later Provost of Trinity College, was a regular guest, as were artists, barristers, dramatists, journalists, medical students, Trinity undergraduates, British officers, and girls. Speranza created a theatrical and murky atmosphere; the inside of her house must have been like a fortune-teller's tent. "The rooms, lit by lamps and candles, were shuttered and closely curtained even in the afternoon when the sun was shining out of doors. People would be arriving and leaving continuously, and filling the crowded room to overflowing."[3]

The *Athenaeum* said that Speranza collected all those "whom prudish Dublin had hitherto kept carefully apart. Hers was the first, and for a long time the only 'Bohemian' house in Dublin." "Boozy and boisterous", Lord Alfred Douglas called it, though he'd never been there. The conversation was certainly unusually free; Speranza "would listen to a flood of bawdy talk and lewd jests without turning a hair"; sometimes she would add to the flood. She never checked it. Her two boys played amid the noise and laughter in the candlelit gloom. She spent time with them, on other days; Oscar rememberd her reading to him the early poems of Walt Whitman. She had passionately wanted a girl as her second child, and was once overheard saying that she had treated Oscar "for a whole ten years as if he had been her daughter."

A Miss Henriette Corkran wrote down her impression of the Merrion Square salons. "I've never, before or since," she wrote, "met anyone in the least like Lady Wilde. Altogether, she struck me as an odd mixture of nonsense, with a sprinkling of genius."[4]

SPERANZA

Speranza preferred men. "As a rule I cannot stand girls or women, they are so flimsy, frivolous, feeble in purpose. . . ." Perhaps Miss Corkran was an exception. She promised to invite "a few men of divine instincts and aspirations" to meet Speranza. For, by an act of creative imagination, nobodies were somebodies in the glamourous dusk of Speranza's rooms. "This is Mr. Bryan McGuire, the poet of Killarney": such introductions enhanced the value of all concerned, including that of the hostess who had brought so many talented characters together. Speranza was also a master of an equally effective toplofty dismissiveness: "As for insignificant people, they should only say what they are expected to say, and never talk of themselves, their children, servants, domestic cares, or their ailments, except to the doctor, who is paid for listening simply because society does not in the least care for the insignificant. . . . The constraint of listening to a long story makes the face dull and heavy."[5]

Miss Corkran left a description of Speranza in her mid-thirties, wearing her laurel wreath on her head, as Harry Furniss drew her, on one of her Dublin Saturday afternoons:

> A very tall figure, she looked over six feet high. She wore that day a long crimson silk gown which swept the floor. Her skirt was voluminous; underneath it there must have been two crinolines, for, when she walked, there was a peculiar swaying, swelling movement like that of a vessel at sea . . . Over the crimson were flounces of Limerick lace, and, round what had once been her waist, an Oriental scarf, embroidered with gold, was twisted. Her long, massive handsome face was plastered with white powder; and over her blue-black glossy hair was a crown of laurels. Her throat was bare, so were her arms, but they were covered with quaint jewellery. On her broad chest were fastened a series of large brooches, evidently family portraits, which came down almost as low as the gastronomical region, and gave her the appearance of a perambulating family mausoleum.

Speranza published her views on feminine dress; a literary lady, she said, should not wear corsets—everything should be "untrammelled and unswathed". She herself looked like "a tragedy queen at a suburban theatre," remarked the uncharitable Miss Corkran. It is easy to laugh at Speranza; but she also had doughty qualities, and a defiant dignity. She had need of them in 1864, the year her husband was knighted.

VICTORIA GLENDINNING

"I wonder what Lady Wilde thought of her husband?" wrote old J. B. Yeats to his poet son, in 1921. He remembered the "scandalous trial": "On that occasion Lady Wilde was loyal." What happened was that the susceptible Sir William had become involved with a patient, Mary Josephine Travers, the unmarried daughter of a distinguished medical colleague. After ten years of sentimental friendship, the lady accused Sir William of violating her person in his surgery. (She claimed to have been momentarily unconscious while the offence took place.) Miss Travers then proceeded to persecute the Wildes with letters to the press, pamphlets and broadsheets pushed through letter-boxes, demonstrations and placards in the streets. Speranza, exasperated, wrote to Miss Travers's father complaining of her behavior, Miss Travers took Speranza to court for destroying her reputation. The whole squalid tale was spread over the Irish and English newspapers.

Miss Travers was clearly unhinged; but Sir William had been, to say the least, unwise. Over the years he had sent the girl money, bought her clothes—including underclothes—and had written letters to her. He did not appear in court; at this juncture one sees the force of Frank Harris's description of him as a "pithecoid person of extraordinary sensuality and cowardice." Speranza, on the other hand, behaved superbly, saying in court that she was "not interested" in the intrigue, only in the nuisance. Miss Travers was awarded damages of one farthing, and costs that, unluckily for the Wildes, came to £2,000.

Meanwhile, the Saturday salons continued. Sir William never attended them anyway, but the case gave ammunition to the mockers. Harry Furniss described the Wildes in their middle age, after the trial:

> Lady Wilde, had she been cleaned up and plainly and rationally dressed, would have made a remarkable fine model of the *Grande Dame*, but with all her paint and tinsel and tawdry tragedy-queen get-up she was a walking burlesque of motherhood. Her husband resembled a monkey, a miserable-looking little creature, who, apparently unshorn and unkempt, looked as if he had been rolling in the dust . . . Opposite to their pretentious dwelling in Dublin were the Turkish baths, but to all appearances neither Sir William nor his wife walked across the street.[6]

Yet he was a successful professional man; and they both

SPERANZA

appeared in good society. As Furniss said, "at all the public functions these two peculiar objects appeared in their dust and eccentricity."

Sex, apparently, did not play a very large part in Lady Wilde's life. Sir William's infidelity was something she was used to. Her passions went into the projection of her social and literary self, and into her sons, whom she loved unconditionally. But she was loyal beyond the call of duty; after her husband died, she finished his memoir of the archaeologist Gabriel Beranger and contributed a preface in glowing tribute to Sir William's memory. While he lay dying, she allowed a veiled woman, the mother of two of his natural children, to come daily and sit silently at his bedside.

Sir William died in 1876, leaving little but debts. When the bailiffs arrived, Speranza took no notice; she lay on the drawing-room sofa and read Aeschylus. After the debts had been paid, and No. 1 Merrion Square sold to Wilde's natural son Dr. Henry Wilson, Speranza, then in her mid-fifties, moved to fresh fields. Willie was in London, working as a journalist. Oscar was at Magdalen College, Oxford. Speranza came to England. To a London journalist Lady Wilde said:

> When we lived in Dublin my receptions in Merrion Square were attended by men and women of recognized position in the worlds of literature and art. On this account they called me an Irish Madame Récamier. Well, while this was flattering, it was perhaps going a little too far. Still, I did endeavour to have something in the nature of a salon. As you are doubtless aware, I am doing the same thing here, but on a smaller scale, at my house in Park Street.

When she first came to London, Speranza lived with her son Willie at No. 1 Ovington square in South Kensington; Oscar was in rooms at 13 Salisbury Street, off the Strand. No sooner had Speranza moved in than she started sending out invitations. Oscar helped her, writing to a Balliol friend: "Any Saturday you are in London I hope you will call and see my mother who is always at home from five to seven on Saturday. She is always glad to see my friends, and usually some good literary and artistic people take tea with her."[7]

By 1880 she had moved to a better address, 116 Park Street, in Mayfair. Although the rooms were smaller than those at No. 1 Merrion Square, she re-established the atmosphere—drawn blinds, closed shutters, red-shaded candles. Older now, she sat on a throne, and held forth. She and Willie sent out cards to everyone

VICTORIA GLENDINNING

they could think of. Arthur Ransome said she was "prepared to suffer fools gladly for the sake of social adulation." Browning came, once. Lillie Langtry, once. Ruskin, once. Nevertheless the salon did so well that she took to opening her doors and closing her shutters twice a week instead of just on Saturdays. The young G. B. Shaw came, gratefully at first: "Lady Wilde was nice to me in the desperate days" (before he started making money). After two or three visits: "I cut myself contemptuously loose from everything of which her at-homes—themselves desperate affairs enough . . . were part."

Shaw, incidentally, had a theory about Speranza's massive physique: he thought she might have suffered from a condition called gigantism. There was something "not quite normal" about Oscar's bigness; and Lady Wilde's hands were enormous . . . and the gigantic splaying of her palm was reproduced in her lumbar region." Through his mother, Shaw thought, Oscar may have been a giant "in the pathological sense".[8]

Oscar was at his best at his mother's Park Street salon: agreeable, supportive, graceful, and as nearly natural as it was possible for him to be, passing the teacups round and being nice to nonentities. The artist Louis Jopling noted his "proud and devoted tone as he introduced people to 'my mother'". As his fame grew, he was the great draw at her parties. Photographs of him were on display all around the room; and, when he came in, he took his place, as the Irish poet Katharine Tynan said, "under the limelight". Meanwhile, his mother was becoming increasingly odd-looking. She was heavily rouged, sometimes wearing a heavy white veil close to her face like a mask. She was also becoming more of a monologuist, expecting the company to listen to her views on life and literature and, often, on the significance of brilliant, cultured women in social life, and the special gifts of specially gifted hostesses. However embarrassing, self-inflating or self-indulgent she was, there is no record of Oscar saying anything sharper than "Ah, come now, mother!"

Willie, too, was cooperative and genial. "Oh, Willie's all right," Speranza had said when they were boys. "He has a first-class brain—but as for Oscar, he will turn out something wonderful!" Willie wrote for the *World* and the *Daily Telegraph*, mostly from a table at the Café Royal with a bottle of brandy at hand. At one time he was dramatic critic for *Punch*; he must have been able. Luther Munday, who lived opposite the Wildes in Park Street, described

Willie as "impulsive, slovenly in person and dress, generous, witty, kindhearted to a fault, unconventional and full of courtesy, a stranger to all pedantry and posing, and a born journalist".[9] He had edited a literary magazine at Trinity College, Dublin; he had been called to the Irish Bar. He was amiable and intelligent.

The trouble seems to have been his character—feckless, irresponsible, immature. He became engaged to the seventeen-year-old Ethel Smyth once on the train from Holyhead to Euston, and then swore her to perpetual secrecy. He cadged money off his mother all the time; he "sponged off everyone but himself," said Oscar. (Willie, in return, said "Thank God my vices are decent.") When Willie married a rich American widow, Mrs. Frank Leslie, Speranza was relieved and delighted; but it did not last. ("No good to me by day or night," said the lady.) Max Beerbohm was cruel, but perhaps right, about Willie, saying he was "nearly as amusing as Oscar but without his charm":

> *Quel monstre*: Dark, oily, suspect yet awfully like Oscar: he has Oscar's coy, carnal smile and fatuous giggle and not a little of Oscar's esprit. But he is awful—a veritable tragedy of family likeness.[10]

As Oscar grew more and more famous and successful, Speranza's star waned. To earn money, she had kept on writing—articles, poems, and a dozen books. She wrote fluently and floridly, as she talked. (Yeats admired her forklore studies.) She had not been taken up in Women's studies, but she was an early and natural feminist, and some of her theories were nicely pungent and, for their time, courageous. "A Joan of Arc was never meant for marriage," she wrote to a friend after Oscar's birth. "And so here I am, bound heart and soul to the home hearth." In an article: "One grows weary of the woeful uniformity of female life and bondage all over the world. . . . Fetters and manacles are on all, for law, prejudice and custom have combined to hold a woman in abject bondage for six thousand years." She suggested the institution of an Order of Merit for women eminent in art and literature; she was outraged, too, that women were "not even represented in the legislature". "The woman of the future," she announced, "will never again be the mere idol of a vain worship", but "man's equal and co-worker".[11]

Poor Speranza was shackled not by any man's "vain worship" but by common poverty. In 1888 Oscar got her a grant of £100 from the Literary Fund; he was also instrumental in getting her a Civil List

VICTORIA GLENDINNING

pension of £70 a year "for services to literature". But it wasn't enough. One of her fondest friends, the American-born Comtesse de Bremont, had noticed that the knocker on the door of 116 Park Street was unpolished, "rusty"; the Irish maid who opened the door was likewise, though very welcoming.

It is probable that the Park Street rent was not being paid; at any rate, in the late 1880s, when Speranza was in her mid-sixties, she moved with her Irish servant to Oakley Street in Chelsea, to what was then No. 146. Both her sons were married, though Oscar and his wife Constance, whom Speranza loved and pitied (Oscar neglected her so) were not far away, in Tite Street.

The Oakley Street house was even smaller than 116 Park Street, and Speranza herself was getting larger and larger. She kept up her Saturday salons. At the beginning they were as crowded as ever, even if the guests were less distinguished. The Comtesse de Bremont attended loyally:

> The door at the top of the flight of steps was wide open. No servant being there to announce me, I followed the stream of callers. A difficult task, as the narrow hall was quite packed. . . . Finally I reached the door of the reception room, and stood there, unable to advance or recede.

When her eyes grew used to the gloom the Comtesse made out the figure of her hostess: "In the semi-darkness Lady Wilde loomed up majestically, her headdress, with its long streamers and glittering jewels, giving her a queenly air." The guests included "long-haired poets and short-haired novelists, smartly dressed Press women, and not a few richly gowned ladies of fashion". The Comtesse was moved by Speranza's "pathetic expression . . . and the evidences of womanly coquetry in the arrangement of her hair, and all those little aids to cheat time and retain a fading beauty".

Another guest, Catherine Hamilton, who went along one December Saturday in 1889, observed that Speranza had not lost the art "de faire un salon". She could still make her guests comfortable and happy. "What matter that the rooms were small, that the tea was overdrawn, or that there was a large hole in the red curtains? Here was a woman who understood the art of entertaining. . . . Thoroughly sympathetic, she entered into the aspirations of everyone who ever held a pen or touched a paintbrush."[12]

SPERANZA

The hole in the curtain was a presage of worse to come. The throng of visitors ebbed unaccountably. Out of the season, when Speranza mistakenly kept her salon open, almost no one came, and those that did were mainly lonely Irish expatriates. The young Yeats was one of them: "the handful of callers contrasts mournfully with the roomful of clever people one meets there in the season." Yet this gave him the opportunity to hear her talk, "and London has few better talkers". "When one listens to her and remembers that Sir William Wilde was in his day a famous *raconteur*, one finds it in no way wonderful that Oscar Wilde should be the most finished talker of our time."[13] Patriotism still burned within her; Frank Harris heard her holding forth in Oakley Street on Parnell as "the man of destiny", who would strike off the fetters and free Ireland, and throne her as Queen among the nations." (This hope, like so many of Speranza's, was to be shattered within months: Parnell was in disgrace by 1890, and in his grave by October 1891.) Speranza still longed, Yeats said, "though certainly among much self-mockery, for some impossible splendour of character and circumstance."

It was not to be. Even the Comtesse de Bremont had noticed "a subtle change in the atmosphere of the dim old room. . . . There was no longer the joyous spirit of intellectual *camaraderie* that had made the dingy surroundings bright with the interchange of wit. Lady Wilde no longer shone forth in her wonderful brilliant manner."

Another American visitor, the novelist Gertrude Atherton, was more outspoken. She wrote of visiting Speranza in "a tiny house in an obscure street" (which is a little unfair to Oakley Street) and went on:

> The gas was presumably turned off, for the hall was pitch dark, and the drawing-room—some eight feet square—into which the miserable slavey conducted us, was lit by three tallow candles. But the strange figure that rose as we entered received us with the grand air. . . . In her day she must have been a beautiful and stately woman; she was still stately, heaven knew, but her old face was gaunt and grey, and seamed with a million criss-crossed lines; etched by care, sorrow, and, no doubt, hunger. Her dress was a relic of the sixties, gray satin trimmed with ragged black fringe over a large hoop-skirt. As her hair was black, it was probably a wig. . . .[14]

This is a glimpse of Speranza off-stage, unpainted, vulnerable: it was not a Saturday. Gertrude Atherton's companion on this visit was

VICTORIA GLENDINNING

the malicious Miss Corkran of Dublin days. One is not surprised to find that no one had married her. The two women had brought Speranza a cake: "She received it gratefully, but put it aside without a glance. Poor thing, no doubt she devoured it whole as soon as we left."

> The room was close and stuffy, the furniture as antiquated as herself; the springs could not have been mended for forty years. She talked to Henriette [Corkran] in a weak quavering voice, mainly of the triumphs of her exalted son, though she drifted back to the past when she had been one of the lights of Dublin with her literary and political salon . . . But to her present circumstances she made no allusion, and the walls seemed to expand until the dingy parlor became a great salon crowded with courtiers, and the rotten fabric of her rag-bag covering turned by a fairy's wand into cloth of gold.

But the dream faded: "Once more she was a laboriously built-up old woman who subsisted mainly on indigestible cake contributed by the few friends who remembered her existence."

The saddest thing of all was that "her exalted son" Oscar stopped coming to her vestigial salons. "I see very little of him," she told Gertrude Atherton. "He is so very busy." And to the Comtesse de Bremont she made an excuse: "Oscar does not come when I have pople here. He is so very much in demand everywhere and he prefers to come when I am alone, as he has so little time now for me that he wishes to have me all to himself."

Oscar was still devoted to Speranza—or rather, to his idea of her. He always romanticized, as she did, her past, exaggerating to his friends the grandeur of her origins and early life in Ireland. "You would imagine from his manner," wrote spiteful Alfred Douglas, "that she was a *grande dame* of the first water with two or three large places to her name and retinues of servants." The first five years of the 1890s were years of fame and fortune for Oscar; he was making about £10,000 a year just before the disaster, while his mother, eccentric, underfed and lonely, sat in the dark in Oakley Street—a reality that tallied ill with his picture of her as ranking "intellectually with Elizabeth Barrett Browning and historically with Madame Roland". Perhaps it was just easier not to go to Oakley Street too often.

Speranza frequented the pawnshop; she sold off some of her books. But even that she did with style; she received the book dealer from her throne and told him with *hauteur* that she would accept "whatever you wish to offer". Oscar did pay her rent, by cheque direct to the landlady; while Speranza herself haggled with the landlady about dirt and damage, which included greasespots on the carpets.

D. J. O'Donoghue, compiler of the *Dictionary of Irish Poets*, went to Oakley Street in the last days, commenting, as everyone did, on the "general tawdriness . . . which the dimmed light quite failed to conceal". "And when", he wrote, "later on, the crash came, everyone who knew them sympathized most with the mother, who was so inordinately proud of her son, and the expression one heard most frequently was, 'Poor Lady Wilde'."[15]

Oscar was arrested in 1895. When he was released on bail in May, no hotel would take him in; he crept to his mother in Oakley Street. His brother Willie, broke as usual, was living there with his second wife (a Miss Lees from Dublin). When Yeats called with letters of sympathy and support for Oscar, it was Willie who received him, embarrassingly drunk and garrulous. During the trial Oscar said: "My poor brother writes to me that he is defending me all over London; my poor, dear brother, he could compromise a steam-engine!"

And "poor Lady Wilde"? She was, as her *Athenaeum* obituary said, now "assailed by misfortunes for which the only sympathy was silence". Her loyalty, as in earlier family crises, was unshaken. It is said she insisted on believing in Oscar's innocence; the truth is, for her he was innocent no matter what he did. In August 1895, when Oscar was in Wandsworth Gaol, she received news of him through Ernest Leverson, and was grateful. "I myself", she wrote to Mr. Leverson, "am very poorly and unable to leave my room." She had hoped to hear from Oscar himself; "but I have not had a line from him, and I have not written to him as I dread my letters being returned." Earlier, before the trial, when some of his friends were urging him to leave the country, she said to him: "If you stay, even if you go to prison, you will always be my son, it will make no difference to my affection, but if you go, I will never speak to you again."[16] Speranza to the last was what Gertrude Atherton called "a leaning tower of courage". She was a woman of great heroism, great dottiness, and great originality, and she believed that she and those she loved were not subject to the ordinary rules. Oscar would not have been Oscar without the qualities he had inherited from her. It may be argued that notoriety itself was a virtue in Speranza's eyes: she was the woman who, in her Merrion Square days, had said

VICTORIA GLENDINNING

to someone desiring to bring a "respectable young woman" to her salon, "You must never use that description in this house. Only tradespeople are respectable. We are above respectability." Yet Oscar's tragedy was too heavy for his mother to bear; the respectables won the day.

Speranza was poor and old and afraid. Editors no longer wanted her articles. She turned to spiritualism, but was soon disillusioned. In early 1896 she got bronchitis; on February 3 she died. Oscar's wife Constance, who was in Genoa at the time, came home, went down to Reading Gaol on February 19 and broke the news to Oscar herself. He believed it was his disgrace that had hastened her end.

Her funeral, which cost £41 5s, was a sparse and spartan affair in Kensal Green cemetery. Her son Willie circulated an In Memoriam card, getting her name wrong. Neither he nor anyone else provided a permanent monument for her in the cemetery, so, after seven years, her remains were transferred to a common, unmarked grave. Willie Wilde died only three years after his mother, and the year after his death Oscar died in exile. The party was over.

Notes

1. Anna, Comtesse de Bremont, *Oscar Wilde and His Mother: a Memoir* (London: Everett, 1911). (Other quotations by the Comtesse de Bremont are from the same book.)
2. Brian de Breffny, "Speranza's Ancestry; Elgee, the Maternal Lineage of Oscar Wilde". *The Irish Ancestor*, Vol. IV, No. 2, 1972.
3. Horace Wyndham, *Speranza* (London: Boardman, 1951).
4. Henriette Corkran, *Celebrities and I* (London: Hutchinson, 1902). (Other quotations by Miss Corkran are from the same book.)
5. Terence de Vere White, *The Parents of Oscar Wilde* (London: Hodder and Stoughton, 1967).
6. Harry Furniss, *Some Victorian Women* (London: John Lane, 1923).
7. Rupert Hart-Davis, ed., *The Letters of Oscar Wilde* (London: Rupert Hart-Davis, 1962).
8. Letter from Shaw in Frank Harris, *Oscar Wilde: His Life and Confessions* (New York: Crown Publishing Co., 1930).
9. Luther Munday, *A Chronicle of Friendship* (London: T. Werner Laurie, 1912).
10. David Cecil, *Max* (London: Constable, 1964).
11. Wyndham, *Speranza*.

SPERANZA

114

12. *Idem.*

13. W. B. Yeats, *Autobiographies* (London: Macmillan, 1955).

14. Gertrude Atherton, *The Adventures of a Novelist* (London, Cape, 1932).

15. D. J. O'Donoghue, *The Irish Book Lover*, Vol. XII, 1921.

16. Yeats, *Autobiographies.*

VICTORIA GLENDINNING

LADY DESBOROUGH

The Souls of London

Max Egremont

On July 10, 1889, George Curzon, then a young bachelor with political ambitions, gave a dinner at the Bachelors' Club in Hamilton Place before leaving London for Switzerland. To the guests he wrote a poem of welcome that contrived to mention each of them in turn (there were to be about forty people present). It began:

> Ho! list to a lay
> Of that company gay
> Compounded of gallants and graces
> Who gathered to dine
> In the year '89,
> In a haunt that in Hamilton Place is.

> There, there where they met
> And the banquet was set
> At the bidding of Georgius Curzon;
> Brave you! 'tis his pride,
> When he errs, that the side
> Of respectable licence he errs on.

> Around him that night—
> Was there e'er such a sight?
> Souls sparkled and spirits expanded;
> For of them critics sang,
> That tho' christened the Gang
> By a spiritual link they were banded.

Souls and spirits no doubt,
But neither without
Fair visible temples to dwell in!
E'en your image divine
Must be girl with a shrine
For the pious to linger a spell in.

The facetious and mock-heroic style of the verses is a suitable introduction to the social group they celebrate; for this was the "Souls", a collection of high-born people who formed a clique in the last years of the nineteenth century. Those present at Curzon's dinner included Arthur Balfour, the Dukes of Sutherland and Rutland and their wives, Lord and Lady Pembroke, Lord and Lady Elcho, Lord and Lady Ribblesdale, Mr. and Mrs. Willie Grenfell, Harry Cust and Margot Tennant. Most were rich (usually by inheritance) and aristocratic. Some of them, like Balfour, were clever as well; and those who were not, knew how to admire the ones who were.

The forming of the "Souls" occurred, according to Margot Asquith (previously Tennant), when her sister Laura, who was married to Alfred Lyttelton, died and their friends went into mourning and saw scarcely anybody except those within their own small circle. They began to value their exclusivity, to pride themselves that their amusements were more worthwhile than those of the rest of their class. At that time, aristocratic pleasures were invariably philistine, consisting of the same yearly slaughter of birds and foxes along with horse-racing, another popular diversion. The Prince of Wales, later Edward VII, set the tone at Newmarket, Ascot or the great country-houses, and in London during the summer—gambling and card-playing, sitting through endless dinners, indulging in clumsy flirtations, oblivious to artistic achievement or beauty.

The "Souls" believed themselves different. Their name itself speaks not only of an ostentatious concern with the mind but also of a romantic delight in fine feeling. It was Admiral Lord Charles Beresford, the friend of the Prince of Wales, who christened them at a dinner party given by Lady Brownlow in 1887, when he announced that, as they always seemed to be talking about their souls, that was what they collectively should be called. The more traditional members of their class were surprised that they preferred lawn tennis to hunting and shooting, enjoyed conversa-

MAX EGREMONT

tion, after-dinner acting and quiz games more than cards, and appeared almost aggressively well-informed about literature and art.

While there was no denying the intellect of Balfour or Curzon, some of the female "Souls" came in for mockery from intelligent observers. In 1892, the poet Wilfrid Scawen Blunt lunched at 11 Downing Street with Sir William Harcourt, the Liberal Chancellor of the Exchequer; and they discussed a rumour that Margot Tennant and others were thinking of publishing a newspaper to give vent to their literary aspirations. "Great joking," noted Blunt, "by Sir William about the 'Souls' journal. I suggested as a motto for it, 'solus cum sola', with an armorial coat, bearing two flat fish osculant all proper. 'Ah,' he said, 'it is their bodies that I like, and now they are going to show us their souls all naked in print, I shall not care for them.' "

In the clique's early years, Margot Tennant was perhaps its most vigorous female member; but in 1894, she married Asquith and, although she remained close to her old friends, had not so much time for social maneuvres. Margot did not possess a country-house near enough to London or sufficiently large to set herself up as a great entertainer of the "Souls": country-house visits, often from Saturday to Monday, provided the ideal background to their amusements. For Balfour, perhaps their central and most admired figure, sport was important; this also applied to many of his associates. Chief among their sports were lawn tennis and golf. Other leisure activities, such as bicycling and, later, motoring, depended on the availability of uncluttered, secluded surroundings—the "fair visible temples" of Curzon's poem. Among those who provided these amenities was Mrs. Willie Grenfell, later Lady Desborough.

Mrs. Grenfell was born Ethel (soon shortened to Etty) Priscilla Fane in 1867, daughter of the Hon. Julian Fane (younger son of the Earl of Westmorland) and Lady Adine Fane (daughter of Earl Cowper). Miss Fane's childhood was lonely. Julian Fane, a diplomat, served briefly as First Secretary in the Paris embassy; by the time Etty was four, both he and her mother had died, leaving her and her brother Johnnie to be brought up by their grandparents. Then Johnnie died when Etty was eight, and her favourite grandmother, Lady Cowper, when the child was thirteen. Henceforth, the uncle and aunt, the new Lord and Lady Cowper, were her closest mentors, and they introduced her to London society. Lord Cowper was a politician, once Lord Lieutenant of Ireland, and his brother Henry a Liberal Member of Parliament. At the Cowper country-house, Panshanger in Hertfordshire, and in London, Miss Fane met Arthur Balfour, Alfred Lyttelton, John Morley and other prominent young figures of the day.

Her marriage, in 1887, was not to one of these men. Willie Grenfell owned a large Victorian house and estate at Taplow in Buckinghamshire on the banks of the Thames. His father had died when Grenfell was a boy; so the property was already his by inheritance. Grenfell had won a scholarship to Balliol, but was more renowned for his sporting skill than for his intelligence. He shot big game in Africa, partridges and pheasants in England, grouse in Scotland, elephants in India and was amateur punting champion three years running and stroked a racing eight across the Channel. He also found time, however, to sit as as Liberal Member of Parliament from 1882 to 1886, and as a Conservative (he had parted from Gladstone over the second Home Rule bill) from 1900 to 1905. In politics, Grenfell's obsession was bimetallism, or the desirability of introducing both gold and silver currencies into the economy; he sat on countless committees devoted to furthering this cause. In 1905, he was created Lord Desborough for his services; the Prime Minister, Arthur Balfour, was perhaps also remembering with gratitude his own frequent visits to Taplow.

Grenfell seems to have played little part in his wife's entertainments. There were jokes about guests being forced to listen to long involved accounts of the advantages of bimetallism after dinner; but Grenfell was no fool. It is probable that he preferred silence to competitive conversation, respecting Etty's gifts as a hostess, understanding her pleasure in these gatherings, even if they were not entirely to his own taste. Often he was away on hunting expeditions or serving on the boards of international sporting bodies. When they were together at Taplow, his wife took pride in their united and happy family life.

Mrs. Sidney Webb felt that Lady Desborough's real aptitude was for administration, noting that she might have made an excellent head of a government department. But her role at Taplow and, later, Panshanger (which she inherited from her aunt in 1914) was primarily that of a catalyst, bringing people together, providing a setting and unobtrusive encouragement, arranging a performance. Balfour, Curzon, and others felt at ease with her; the "Souls" became expansive and members competed, under her roof, for the

MAX EGREMONT

honour of appearing the most brilliant performer, the most outstanding guest. Her presence could be both comforting and inspiring, pleasing and alarming. A young man, who recorded his impressions of her after the First World War, wrote of "her disconcerting habit of suddenly concentrating her strong character on you", and then noticing that, "in spite of the alarm", she was making you laugh. "And then I found I was being very amusing myself." He noted that "later, I discovered this was her great gift. She herself was not only brilliant in conversation, but she made everyone else feel brilliant."

Charm, a striking personal presence, the ability to lead a conversation: these seem to have been Lady Desborough's talents. She was a hostess, the impresario of Taplow who knew how to arrange her guests into the position, the mood, the social state that most flattered them, and indirectly herself. Frivolity was generally the predominant public tone, with intensity of feeling reserved for the privacy of personal relationships. There was no great desire to startle or to shock; for, if the "Souls" were rebels, their rebellion was of the most gentle kind. Those in the small clique at their centre were all from the same privileged background; and, if they prided themselves on their acquaintance with Oscar Wilde and later H. G. Wells, their intimate friendships were all with those of their own class, conducted against a magnificence often at least the equal of that enjoyed by the despised philistines of the Prince of Wales's set. Taplow was equipped with a full retinue of servants and every comfort the age could provide. "My dear Brodrick," John Morley remarked to his friend on leaving a gathering of the "Souls", "these two days have been delightful, but most blighting to one's democracy."

The "Souls", when the challenge came, had no doubt where their loyalties lay. In the easy political concourse of the 1880s, Liberals and Conservatives mingled easily at social gatherings. Then Home Rule began a slow hardening of attitudes, with many aristocratic Liberals, like Grenfell, deserting Gladstone over the Irish Question. The Conservative defeat of 1906 was followed by Lloyd George's budget of 1909, which declared war on the property-owning classes by introducing a land tax, and by the Ulster crisis, which brought Home Rulers and Unionists close to civil war. Faced with these reverses, the "Souls" united with the class compatriots they had once mocked to fight a rear guard action, some, like George Wyndham, even hopelessly plotting an aristocratic revolution

LADY DESBOROUGH

against Asquith's measures to curb the power of the House of Lords. In this climate, Margot Asquith complained that her old friends cut her at parties or rudely attacked her for her husband's policies. Suddenly, their lives seemed to be constructed on shifting sands rather than on the old firm base one might laughingly tilt against, yet, mercifully, never hope to destroy.

In the early days, a self-congratulatory simplicity was one of the features of the "Souls" mild rebellion. They would go on bicycling trips through France, while their maids and valets followed by train, and speak with disdain of vast country-house shooting parties where the comfort was lavish, but the conversation dim. Behind this lay the firm belief that their sensibilities were on a more elevated plane than those of most of their contemporaries, that their interests were wider and more worthwhile. Compared with their other class associates, they were indeed generally more intelligent, more receptive to ideas, more interested in literature and the arts. Yet, if taken in a wider European context, their experience today seems secluded and their approach unadventurous. Their favourite writers were William Morris and Maurice Baring. The artists they admired were Burne-Jones, Sargent and Watts; they enjoyed the music of Elgar and Sir Hubert Parry, with its sometimes crude expression of late-Victorian confidence and optimism. They liked Morris for his medieval romances, rather than for his utopian political views, Baring for his extraordinary facility for literary imitation of a clever, but ultimately hollow kind. Occasionally, this admiration for the grandiose and the frivolous resulted in fanciful absurdity.

This absurdity could reveal itself in their communications with each other. It is important to remember that Lady Desborough and her friends had ample leisure to explore in detail the tergiversations of their personal feelings; and this often gave rise to a lushness of expression that might have been tempered by a more humdrum existence. Friendships between "Souls" of different sexes were not always sexual affairs, but were apt to develop into romances where emotion, at least, was unrestricted. In the early 1890s, Etty corresponded with George Wyndham, a young Conservative Member of Parliament and protégé of Arthur Balfour. Wyndham was almost a caricature of a masculine "Soul"—handsome, poetic, gifted with literary and conversational fluency, a young Tory with a romantic conception of his country's imperial mission. Once, while staying with his cousin Wilfrid Scawen Blunt, he wrote a long poem

MAX EGREMONT

in complicated metre while resting for an hour between sets of tennis. Such facile brilliance immediately marked him for attention and success at Taplow.

At first, Wyndham's future seemed assured, and his confidence was only equalled by his romanticism. In 1892, he addressed Etty as "Dear April", "for so I must be allowed to call you," he wrote. "April you have been and must ever be! An April of sunshine and no rain: of laughter and no tears; all radiant and dazzling blossoms robbed from May. Please remember always to be April and to refuse anything but flowers." His political career took him first to a minor post at the War Office and then, in 1900, to the demanding, almost impossible, job of Chief Secretary for Ireland. Lord Salisbury, Prime Minister and the very antithesis of a "Soul", might remark of him "I don't like poets," but Wyndham, with the support of Balfour, was spoken of as a possible future Conservative leader. Then, in 1905, with a suspicion among Unionists that he had allowed his Permanent Under-Secretary to become involved in a scheme of devolution for Irish government, Wyndham came under attack from his own party. He collapsed with a nervous breakdown, resigned, and drifted into an unhappy decline.

Balfour's prime ministership marked the political apogee of the "Souls", also the beginning of the slow breakup of their secure, self-confident world. To some, his government seemed unnecessarily incestuous. His brother Gerald was at the Board of Trade; his friends Brodrick, Wyndham and Alfred Lyttelton at the India Office, the Irish Office, and the Colonial Office; his cousin, the new Lord Salisbury, became Lord Privy Seal; and Lord Curzon continued as Viceroy. (All these were visitors to Taplow.) But almost as soon as the government was formed, it began to disintegrate. Curzon had a terrible quarrel with Brodrick about Indian administration and resigned; Wyndham collapsed; Lyttelton proved a poor performer in the House of Commons; and Joseph Chamberlain's campaign for tariff reform hopelessly split the Conservatives, with his supporters on one side, immovable free traders like Salisbury and his Cecil brothers on the other, and Balfour trying to gather together some form of compromise in the middle.

In 1906, the Conservatives suffered the worst electoral defeat in recent British history. Balfour continued as leader in opposition, but the party was still divided, and his conciliatory tactics satisfied neither side. The Lloyd George budget of 1909 and Asquith's Parliament Bill exacerbated the divisions; some Tories wished to use the House of Lords to destroy both measures; others were more cautious. In August 1911, the Parliament Bill, whose aim was to curb the veto power of the Lords, was passed by the Peers with the help of moderate Conservatives, led by Curzon and supported by Balfour, against the fury of diehards such as George Wyndham and the Cecils. Amid the fierceness of factional feeling, the old gentility of the "Souls" was forgotten. "I will never," Wyndham wrote to his wife, "meet Curzon at a council convened by Balfour. . . .Now we are finished with the cosmopolitan press—and the American duchesses and the Saturday to Mondays at Taplow— and all the degrading shams."

In November, Balfour resigned as leader of the Conservatives and was succeeded by Andrew Bonar Law, a dour Presbyterian committed to a loyal Ulster and tariff reform. Balfour had been the leading figure of the "Souls", their centre of admiration and most satisfying source of praise. Yet, through his remarkable powers of detachment, he had never allowed himself to become wholly involved in their fantasies or rituals of affection. His letters to Lady Desborough are restrained and informative, entirely free from the romantic excesses of Wyndham or many of her other male correspondents; hers to him are full of tentative enquiries about books and philosophy, often self-conscious and tightly phrased, as if she were afraid to relax lest some sign of foolishness be revealed. Balfour was a philosopher as well as a politician. Here his work was devoted largely to an attempted reconciliation of religion with science, a quest he followed all his active life. In 1895, he published "The Foundations of Belief" about which Reginald Brett, later Lord Esher, noted: "It is really hard when you are the apostle of a charming sect, to trouble their minds with abstract speculation. . . .However, Mrs. Grenfell and the others will no doubt feel that no one is likely to tackle them about details—so they can pretend to know all about it." Curzon wrote in 1889 about Balfour in his poem of welcome:

There was seen at that feast
Of this band, the High Priest,
The heart that to all hearts is nearest;
Him may nobody steal
From the true Common weal
Tho' to each is dear Arthur the dearest.

Balfour and Curzon, both frequent visitors to Taplow, were

MAX EGREMONT

perhaps the most distinguished of the "Souls". Lady Desborough must, however, have found their social approach and manners very different. Balfour enjoyed the subtle interchange of general conversation and was a receptive listener, but always rather distant in personal relationships; Curzon preferred the monologue, was a fiercely competitive talker, and relished amorous pursuit and sexual conquest; the fastidious Balfour liked philosophical discussion and fended off intimacies. Curzon was at home in the masculine gatherings of Wilfrid Scawen Blunt's Crabbet Club, which met at Crabbet Park (Blunt's house in Sussex), its members sitting up most of the summer night drinking through impromptu speeches and recitations, then breaking off at dawn to swim and play tennis naked. At first, in the salons of the "Souls", they were friends, but quarrelled when Balfour, as Prime Minister, refused to accede to demands made by Curzon as Viceroy. In 1923, one of the reasons Curzon did not succeed Bonar Law as Prime Minister was because Balfour advised George V to choose Baldwin.

To some, who saw only the affected, nonchalant exterior and not the iron-like toughness beneath, Balfour's association with the "Souls" exemplified a preciosity and languid refinement that they found distasteful and could not always understand. Many traditional Tories of the squirearchy held this view; one of them, Lord Winterton, wrote that the public "did not know exactly what the "Souls" were, but vaguely disapproved of them. Thus, one's supporters would say to one, 'We want a man like good old Joe Chamberlain as leader, not a "Soul" like Balfour.' If you asked them to define a 'Soul' they were silent. It was just something they didn't understand, and, in consequence, disliked and that was that!"

Others believed that the "Souls" were living in a backwater, out of touch with the vigorous world of industry and technology, valuing only the pursuit of beauty, secure with their country estates and inherited wealth. In 1902, Rudyard Kipling, apostle of Joseph Chamberlain's vigorous imperialism, published a satirical fable called "Below the Mill Dam", in which two "Soul-like" characters, the Black Rat and the Grey Cat, sit in a mill complacently discoursing, while the old mill wheel revolves behind them, hissing out the history of the neighbourhood. The Grey Cat yawns, complains of the miller shouting "large and vague threats to my address, last night at tea, that he wasn't going to keep cats who 'caught no mice'. Those were his words. I remember the grammar sticking in my throat like a herring bone." "And what did you do?"

LADY DESBOROUGH

asks the Black Rat, to which the Cat replies, "What does one do when a barbarian utters? One ceases to utter and removes. I removed—towards his pantry. It was a riposte he might appreciate." Eventually, in answer to the clamouring waters of the mill stream, the old wheel is replaced by modern machinery, accepting its fate with delight as a further step in the march of progress. The Rat is caught, stuffed, and put in a glass case by the mill's new engineer, leaving the Grey Cat alone, pathetically congratulating itself that "I, at least, have preserved the spirit of the mill."

Such attacks showed that the "Souls" attracted a certain amount of attention outside their own small aristocratic circle. Lady Desborough probably enjoyed this; but it would be an error to pretend that she herself was a very remarkable figure. If, by unconsciously adding to the legend of Balfour's preciosity, she turned some people against him, it was through no premeditated campaign on her part. The same observer who remarked on her conversational brilliance and ability to make "everyone else seem brilliant" also added that "this was her only gift." Apparently, she knew little of the visual arts and disliked music. She read a great deal, but more from a feeling of duty than for pleasure. She was attractive rather than beautiful; charm and grace were her predominant characteristics—both ideal attributes for a hostess. They were not, however, so appropriate for a mother; it was inevitable that, as socializing occupied so much of her time and energy, her domestic life would suffer.

Nicholas Mosley has written an interesting account of Lady Desborough, her family, and her circle; of this, the major and most absorbing part analyses her relationship with her son Julian Grenfell. Mosley describes Etty's friends, her flirtations, her way of life in detail, demonstrating that they followed an almost monotonous pattern. With men, there seems to be little evidence of passionate or prolonged sexual involvement; instead we find a repetitive game, with its ultimately empty protestations of eternal devotion and an ever-changing set of players. Her eldest son, however, was there the whole time, and this led to complications. At first, they took the form of conventional adolescent rebellion; Julian avoided his mother's friends, refused to go to her parties, mocked her standards and pretensions. Then, while at Oxford, he suffered what seems to have been a minor nervous breakdown, experiencing acute physical and mental lassitude; he channelled his frustrations into a series of essays that attacked the fantasy life of

MAX EGREMONT

the "Souls" and offended his mother. He tried to publish his essays, failed, then joined the army and served in India and South Africa.

The First World War came almost as a relief to Julian for life at the front was simple, with one obvious enemy and plenty of outlets for excess energy. Immediately before its outbreak, he appeared to be drifting back into his mother's orbit; he had been thinking of standing as a Conservative candidate and had been writing her affectionate, amusing letters. From the trenches, he sent her some poems, including the famous "Into Battle". As a brave winner of the D.S.O., he was held up as a fine example throughout the army. In 1915, he died in the hospital from a severe head wound; his mother and father were at his side. Some months later, his brother Billy also died while leading an attack near Ypres.

Afterwords, Lady Desborough enshrined her visualization of her relationship with her children in a book called "A Family Journal". It is primarily a collection of their letters, occasionally doctored to show more affection and devotion than the originals. There can be no doubt that she had adored the boys and showed formidable courage in facing up to their deaths. Yet her complete incomprehension of Julian's early rebellion, her desire (partly fulfilled) that he should develop along the lines she and her friends thought suitable, reveal a rigid conventionality, the "Souls" unadventurous, complacent side. "Into Battle", with its sentimental romanticising of war and death, is similar in spirit to Rupert Brooke's sonnets of 1914; it is a fine work, memorable in phrasing and sharp in execution, but imbued with a fantasy far removed from the brutal realism of Sassoon or Owen. Lady Desborough could be proud that her son had written such lines.

After the war, the salon continued. Panshanger, an eighteenth-century house near Hertford, had been inherited by Lady Desborough from her aunt, Lady Cowper, in 1914 and was an additional place for entertaining. Now the "Souls" were growing old; but the younger generation was invited, sometimes for Lady Desborough's children, often for herself. Occasionally a note of mockery crept in. In 1930, Lytton Strachey came to Taplow and later wrote about a party that included J. M. Barrie and Lord David Cecil. He noted that "Lord Desborough himself was really the best of the crew—a huge old rock of an athlete—almost completely gaga—I spent the whole Sunday afternoon with him tête-à-tête. He showed me his unpublished books—"The History of the Thames", "The History of the Oar", etc., etc. He confessed he had read the whole of Shakespeare—'And you know there is some pretty stiff stuff in him'!"

As time passed and the slump and the second war led to retrenchment, the Desboroughs came to be regarded as curiosities, representatives of another age, to be questioned about the world before 1914 and the changes they had seen. He became chairman of the Thames Conservancy Board and a knight of the Garter, dying at age eighty-nine in 1945. An obituarist wrote, "I do not believe that in his own way there has ever been a greater Englishman". His wife lived on until 1952 at Panshanger, saying to friends of her early days, "We did have such fun, didn't we?" It is perhaps not a bad or unenviable epitaph.

MAX EGREMONT

Jane Francesca Wilde in youth; "an odd mixture
of nonsense with a sprinkling of genius." (21)

...anza in the role of Madame Récamier;
...ature by Harry Furniss. (22)

With her uncouth husband,
Sir William Wilde;
caricature by Harry Furniss. (23)

Mrs. Grenfell in youth; a contemporary photograph. (

Opposite: **Lady Desborough with her two beloved sons.** (

With her friend and fellow
"Soul" Lord Balfour at a
London wedding, 1924. (26)

Mabel Dodge at the Villa Curonia, 1912. (27)

John Reed. (28)

Berthold Viertel, poet and director. (29)

1abery Road. (30)

Karel Capek; "he saw the future as only a poet can see it." (31)

President Masaryk. At meetings of the Fri Group the President sat next to Capek. (3

Prague, across the Vltava River. (33)

he young American heiress from San Francisco. (34)

Grosvenor Square with George Moore; conversation piece by Lavery, 1925. (35)

The ebullient London hostess; photograph by Cecil Beaton. (36)

Sir Thomas Beecham,
1949, one of the pillars
of Lady Cunard's
salon with his trim
Valois beard and his
fruity delivery". (37)

MABEL DODGE

Evenings in New York

Robert A. Rosenstone

Mabel Dodge's salon . . . burst upon New York like a rocket.
Margaret Sanger

It was the only successful salon I have ever seen in America.
Lincoln Steffens

Many famous salons have been established by women of wit or beauty;
Mabel's was the only one ever established by pure willpower.
And it was no second-rate salon;
everybody in the ferment of ideas could be found there.
Max Eastman[1]

Mabel Dodge was rich and attractive and more than a little lucky. For two years—from 1912 to 1914—she was hostess of the most famous, and no doubt the most interesting, salon in American history. This success was no accident, but rather the result of a subtle interplay between her own needs and ambitions and the historical moment. It was a very special period in the cultural life of the United States, for in the brief years before the First World War, America was flooded with ideas that had been developing in Europe for more than a century—the theories of Marx, Freud, Bergson and Nietzsche, the doctrines of syndicalism, anarchism, socialism and naturalism, the visions of Cubists and Fauves.[2] These, when blended with native American movements in politics, art, and social life, formed a volatile, radical Bohemian subculture which produced new styles of living, publications, cultural forms, and institutions. Much of this activity centered in Greenwich Village, and Mabel Dodge's salon became a primary meeting place for the artists, intellectuals, seekers, and radicals who called that region home.

She seems an unlikely hostess for gatherings where public issues, intellectual doctrines, or radical actions were debated. Mabel was a private person who, for most of her life, held as an ideal something she called *"la grande vie intérieure"*. She was a mystic, always on the trail of the infinite, which she often managed to confuse with psychic love, the sexual impulse, or a combination of the two. She was a person whose interest in herself and her own problems was so enormous that she underwent psychoanalysis twice and then wrote nine lengthy volumes of *Intimate Memories* (five of which remain unpublished) as a continuation of the therapeutic process. Finally, she was a rich woman whose idea of getting close to "the people" was to ride in a chauffeur-driven limousine through the ghetto of the Lower East Side or to live in a luxurious mansion amidst the impoverished Indian pueblo-dwellers of Taos, New Mexico.

That Mabel could create such a successful salon tells as much about the era as about her. It was a period when the distinction between inner and outer worlds became fuzzy and blurred. Words such as "liberation", "rebellion", and "revolution" were on everyone's lips in the radical Bohemian subculture of New York, but their meanings ran in two opposite directions, one personal and the other public. The former meant freeing oneself from the dead hand of the past, from those attitudes usually (and erroneously) labeled Puritanism. This was believed to have stifled both artistic and sexual modes of expression and turned America into a drab, joyless, business-like civilization whose citizens were stunted and warped by the pursuit that William James termed "the bitch goddess Success". The latter path meant sympathy for and action on behalf of those other victims, the laboring classes of the industrial order, the men and women whose toil created the vast wealth which they could not enjoy, but which allowed a small minority to control the political, economic, and social destinies of the nation.

The salon got under way just when a revolt against business, industrialism, and narrow definitions of human potential was taking some middle class people from small towns and provincial cities to major urban centers. In communities like Greenwich Village, many people began to live outside the conventions of normal bourgeois

ROBERT A. ROSENSTONE

society. Both men and women sought to define themselves in new ways—they refused to take regular jobs, lived together openly without being married, experimented in various art forms, theorized endlessly about life, drank a good deal, and felt free to seek new forms of insight through the infant practice of psychoanalysis. This self-indulgence and hedonism was tempered by a social conscience. Smatterings came with them from hometowns, where ghosts of the Populist revolt of the nineties still lingered, where village atheists thundered against Christianity, and where the growing Socialist Party—whose candiate Eugene V. Debs was to win almost a million Presidential votes in 1912—had established reading rooms or run candidates for local office. The glaring contrast between rich and poor in the metropolis gave further fuel to notions of exploitation, and the Village itself was a schoolroom full of radical social and political doctrines—the anarchism of Emma Goldman; the syndicalism of Big Bill Haywood, leader of the Industrial Workers of the World; the socialism of Morris Hillquit. In the Village, it was impossible to ignore the lesson that the traditional American parties and labor unions did not cover the full spectrum of political and economic wisdom.

Mabel's road to the Village was unlike those of most of her contemporaries. She had been born Mabel Ganson in 1879, the only child of a wealthy, banking family in the provincial city of Buffalo, New York. It was not an affectionate household, and some of Mabel's earliest memories were of the implacable warfare that can exist between men and women. For the most part, it was a cold war, but sometimes anger broke into the open, and her father raged with an impotent fury, stamping, shouting, and swearing, while her mother hid a "cold, merciless, expressionless contempt behind her book or newspaper."[3] Eventually he would slam out of the room, his angry actions covering what Mabel would interpret as defeat. The lessons from her parents sank deep. All her life, Mabel would see relationships as a struggle for power and dominance, and she would adopt her mother's attitudes—speaking little and asserting her own will through silent manipulation.

She was dimly aware of this behavior which, with regard to men, sometimes rose close to consciousness. Seeing her days as a search for love, Mabel could easily write that "like most women, all my life I . . . needed and longed for the strong man who would take responsibility for me and my decisions. I wanted to lie back and float on the dominating decisive current of an all-knowing, all-under-

MABEL DODGE

standing man." Yet much as she might claim the problem to be that she "had never known any such men," there were moments when she recognized the struggle raged in her own psyche: "Something in us wants men to be strong, mature, and superior to us so that we may admire them, thus consoled in a measure for our enslavement to them. . . . But something else in us wants them to be inferior, and less powerful than ourselves so that obtaining the ascendancy over them we may gain possession not only of them, but of our own souls, once more."[4] What Mabel never admitted was that her relations with women—either as friends, rivals for a man's affection, or in her few homosexual encounters—were marked by the same bitter kind of conflict.

From an early age, the mystic in Mabel saw herself as an essentially passive creature whose actions were guided by the mysterious current of the universe. Outwardly her childhood was normal for her era and social class—private schools, flirtations with boys and girls, a summer on the continent, a fashionable début. But her real life was an inner one. Morbidly sensitive to her own feelings, she lived in an introspective world where emotion was much more highly valued than intellect. She was pulled to her first husband, Karl Evans, not by passion, but because he was already engaged. Tearing him away from another allowed Mabel to glory in her own powers. When he was killed in a hunting accident shortly after their son was born, she soon scandalized Buffalo by engaging in a barely concealed affair with a prominent, married doctor. Public pressure forced this liaison to end and Mabel's mother packed her off to Europe, where, at twenty-two, she fell into the willing arms of Edwin Dodge, an independently wealthy Boston architect.

On her part, it was hardly a love relationship. Before the marriage ceremony in Paris, Mabel informed Dodge that "I wasn't in love with him, and I felt nothing for him except a desire for him to be about, to help me, and to enable me to make something new and beautiful."[5] Soon they were doing just that with the Villa Curonia at Arcetri, perched in the hills overlooking Florence. While Edwin used his professional talents to remodel the villa, his wife took charge of decorating the interiors, devoting days to an endless search for antique furniture, statues, paintings, porcelains, and tapestries. The result was a magnificent setting in which Mabel, attired in flowing robes and silk turbans, played hostess to rich American and British expatriates, members of the Italian nobility, and figures from the world of art—actress Eleanor Dusa, theatrical designer Gordon

ROBERT A. ROSENSTONE

Craig, sculptor Jo Davidson, painter Janet Scudder, and the then unknown writer Gertrude Stein, who produced "Portrait of Mabel Dodge at the Villa Curonia", a work which neglected to mention either the hostess or the villa.

The Villa Curonia was the center of Mabel's life for a decade. Her husband had early on ceased to interest her; Edwin was too limited, proper, dull, and lacking in sophistication—in short, too American. By now contemptuous of her native land—which she saw as devoted to money-grubbing, sordid politics, and brutal sports— Mabel was still too young and vital to live permanently in a museum. Life grew stale and repetitive as the years passed, and increasingly Mabel felt out-of-sorts, weak and sickly. Often she remained in bed for days, and once she attempted suicide. Eventually recognizing that she desperately needed a change, she decided to move to New York City in the fall of 1912. This was a difficult decision. To leave the continent was to abandon the home of "everything worthwhile" in life; to return home was to enter a land of "machinery and factories" that could only be described as "ugly! ugly! ugly!"[6]

At first, New York City lived up to all her fears. She hated the dirt and grime, the nervous crowds of men pursuing "the main chance," the fact that people seemed wholly devoid of an inner life, of spiritual or artistic interests. Her son went off to boarding schools; Edwin opened an office, and Mabel remained sullenly at home—in a large apartment occupying the entire second floor of 23 Fifth Avenue— just a few steps from the edge of Greenwich Village. To relieve the darkness of the city and her mood, she made the rooms as bright as possible. Everything was white—the paper on the walls, paint on the woodwork, linen curtains on the windows, marble mantlepiece, bearskin rug on the floor, silk Chinese shawls draped from the walls of her bedroom, and curtains that served as the canopy of her four-poster bed. In this pristine setting, she placed delicate, pastel, antique chairs and *chaises longue* from France and Italy, mirrors in gilt Renaissance frames, velvet couches with cushions of damask and brocade and Venetian tables and commodes.

This labor served its purpose for a time, but when the job was complete, Mabel felt dreadfully lonely. Now Edwin was worse than boring; his presence seemed to suffocate her. Once again Mabel slipped into depression. She took to bed with headaches, severe colds, tonsillitis. Lying in a darkened room day after day, she began to have mystical experiences. These led to the summoning of psychiatrist Bernard Sachs. Somehow Mabel persuaded him that

MABEL DODGE

her husband was the cause of all her problems, and the dutiful doctor explained to Edwin that his wife could only recover if he stayed away from the apartment for a while. Once he left, Edwin never again came back into Mabel's life.

Her husband's departure helped release Mabel from sickness and lethargy, but there were other factors as well. Even before Edwin left, she had begun to touch the current of Manhattan's cultural life. At a dinner party she had encountered Carl Van Vechten, music critic for the *Times*, a friendly, whimsical, vital sort who quickly became the first person to animate her "lifeless rooms." Then, fresh from Europe, Jo Davidson appeared, and soon he was bringing friends from the worlds of art, journalism, and theater to the white apartment. Here were the first traces of what would eventually become the salon. But before that could happen, Mabel, in the winter of 1912-13, suddenly launched herself wholeheartedly into New York life by taking an active part in one of those epoch-making events by which a new cultural radicalism was to define itself—the Armory Show, which for the first time brought to America the stunning, modernist visions of contemporary European visual arts.

It was an event that confused politics and culture. The artists who organized it, Walter Kuhn and Arthur B. Davies, had chosen the pinetree flag of Massachusetts flown during the American Revolution as the Armory Show's symbol. Supporters like Robert Henri, Alfred Stieglitz, and John Sloan were not only proclaiming the exhibition as a battle cry of freedom for artistic expression, but also calling it a "bomb" under social conventions. Mabel was swept into this atmosphere because of her connection to Gertrude Stein, one of the earliest collectors of Picasso, Matisse, and Braque. Asked to write a piece for a magazine, Mabel connected the verbal experiments of Stein to the visual ones of Picasso and—in her own mystical way—claimed that both were charting new roads along which "consciousness is pursuing truth to eternity."[7]

Words were not her only contribution. In her chauffeur-driven automobile, Mabel helped to gather works from private collections and deliver them to the 69th Street Armory. Then she sent a check for five hundred dollars to the organizers and, with it, a note that read: "Anything that will extend the unawakened consciousness here (or elsewhere) will have my support. . . .The majority are content to browse upon past achievements. What is needed is more, more, and always more consciousness, both in art and in

ROBERT A. ROSENSTONE

life."[8] To these philosophical notions, she added personal and political ones. By now Mabel felt that the Exhibition belonged to her: "It became, overnight, my own little Revolution . . . I was going to dynamite New York and nothing would stop me."[9] To Stein, she feverishly wrote that the show would be "the most important public event. . . .since the signing of the Declaration of Independence, and it is of the same nature. . . .There will be a riot and a revolution, and things will never be quite the same afterwards."[10]

Neither Mabel nor the organizers were to be disappointed. From the moment the Armory show opened on February 17, 1913, it was a center of controversy. Never before had Americans flocked in such numbers to an exhibition or so passionately debated the work of artists. The center of the storm was a small number of European moderns—the Fauves, Cubists, and Expressionists—and it was Marcel Duchamp's "Nude Descending the Staircase" that struck some as verging on lunacy. Humorists might dismiss it as "An Explosion in a Shingle Factory" or "Staircase Descending a Nude", but others took such Cubist visions as a sign of impending doom. No less a reviewer than ex-President Theodore Roosevelt referred to Cubists and Futurists as a "lunatic fringe" of "European extremists."[11] *The New York Times* pointed to more sinister implications:

> This movement is surely part of the general movement, discernible all over the world, to disrupt and degrade, if not destroy, not only art, but literature and society, too. . . . The cubists and futurists are . . . cousins to the anarchists in politics, the poets who defy syntax and decency, and all the would-be destroyers who, with the pretense of trying to regenerate the world, are really trying to block the wheels of progress in every direction.[12]

No better statement of the differences between the custodians of the old culture and the proponents of the new one could be made. The Armory Show had neatly drawn a line between generations—if not chronological, then cultural ones. Both sides could agree that art, literature, politics, and social life were inextricably intertwined, that changes in one went hand in hand with changes in all the others. Yet Mabel's generation reversed the underlying values of the *Times* editorial. Believing it was indeed possible to "regenerate the world," they conceived progress as something that manifested itself in radical change in art forms, life styles, and economic and political power. For Mabel, infatuation with the antique had shifted

MABEL DODGE

to passion for the new; revolutionary doctrines in art and society expressed the mysterious movement of the universe.

By the time the Armory Show had opened and her article on Stein had brought her some notoriety, Mabel's "evenings" were under way. Carl Van Vechten and Jo Davidson's contacts helped draw more people to the white apartment, which seemed always full of poets, music critics, painters, journalists, playwrights, and actors. Meanwhile, she was busy meeting people all over town. Her closest companion and guide was Hutchins Hapgood, a middle-aged journalist whose own mystical streak seemed to make them "soul mates". Hutch, a theoretical anarchist who believed it his "duty to undermine subtly the foundations of the community," had written on radicals, labor unions, ghetto residents, art movements, and love. [13] It was Hapgood who led her to 291, Alfred Stieglitz's avant-garde gallery, where she met painters Marsden Hartley and Andrew Dasburg and first saw the works of John Marin and Georgia O'Keeffe. Hutch also brought Mabel into the presence of genuine, committed radicals, Emma Goldman and her former lover, Alexander Berkman, who had spent fourteen years in jail for the attempted assassination of steel magnate Henry Frick. Mabel was suitably impressed: "They were the kind that *counted*. They had authority. Their judgment was somehow true." [14]

An infatuation with modern art and political movements would give Mabel's salon its special flavor. Yet oddly enough, the first evening had nothing to do with either realm, included no serious conversation, and was a failure, which indicates something about the limitations of the era's radicalism. The architect was Van Vechten, one of the first white intellectuals to take an interest in the culture of black Harlem. When he insisted on bringing two performers to the apartment, Mabel provided an audience. It proved to be an uncomfortable occasion. While a man strummed a banjo and sang off-color songs, a woman in white stockings and black button boots performed a lewd dance. Mabel was shocked: "They both leered and rolled their suggestive eyes and made me feel first hot and then cold, for I never had been so near this kind of thing before." Only Van Vechten seemed to be enjoying himself, and as the woman pulled her skirt higher and higher, members of the crowd began to mutter and avert their eyes. Appalled as anyone, Mabel at least knew how to find consolation: "One must let life express itself in whatever form it will." [15]

ROBERT A. ROSENSTONE

The next idea for the evenings was more acceptable. Already the apartment was a kind of open house, and all it took to launch the salon was a suggestion as to how to organize the freewheeling discussions that were often in progress. Mabel gives credit for this to Lincoln Steffens, who was, like Hapgood, a renowned journalist. A graduate of the University of California and an erstwhile student in Heidelberg, Berlin, and Paris, Steffens had become famous a decade before when he had been one of the original muckrakers on *McLure's Magazine*. He specialized in exposing the corruption of city and state politics, but was too sophisticated to think that political bosses were necessarily bad persons and reformers good ones. Rather, it was human systems which produced evil. The way to improve the world, Steffens believed, was a doctrine called "Christian anarchism," the tenets of which nobody but he could accept. No matter. He loved good food, drink, conversation, and social life, and Mabel's could be a setting for all of those.

She later remembered Steffens's suggestion in a way most flattering to herself. He told her that she had a

> magnetic, social faculty. You attract, stimulate, and soothe people, and men like to sit with you and talk to themselves! You make them think more fluently, and they feel enhanced. If you had lived in Greece long ago, you would have been called a *hetaira*. Now why don't you see what you can do with this gift of yours? Why not organize all this accidental, unplanned activity around you, this coming and going of visitors, and see these people at certain hours. Have 'evenings'!

When Mabel protested that he and Hutch were always warning against the dangers of too much organization, Stef replied:

> Oh, I don't mean that you should *organize* the evenings. I mean, get people here at certain times and let them feel absolutely free to be themselves and see what happens. Let everybody come! All these different kinds of people that you know, together here, without being managed or herded in any way! Why, something wonderful might come of it! You might even revive general conversation![16]

Even if this description, written many years later, is not accurate, it does capture her specific, subtle contribution to the evenings. Mabel did have a rare faculty for attracting people and making them wish to speak from the heart. This was not the result of physical beauty, but manner, spirit, or what she might call "soul". Basically, she was a rather plain woman, short and plump. Yet she had a very definite and unique sense of style, even panache. Mabel did not follow current fashions, but always dressed in long robes and often covered her head with floppy hats, huge turbans, or flowing scarves. The total picture was appealing to men and women alike, and members of both sexes seemed quite regularly to fall in love with her.

Oddly enough for the hostess of a salon, Mabel had few verbal gifts. She could be animated when talking with a good friend alone, but in a group situation, she was neither witty, wise, nor deep. Knowing this, she rarely opened her mouth during the evenings. Still, even in a crowd of a hundred people, her special magic seemed to work. Max Eastman, the *Masses* editor who had little liking for Mabel and none at all for any salon, was impressed by her powers. On seeing that "she sits like a lump and says nothing," he recalled, one might be tempted to "move on to someone else who at least knew how to make conversation." But soon the guest would be back because "there is something going on, or going around, in Mabel's head or bosom, something that creates a magnetic field in which people become polarized and pulled in and made to behave very queerly. Their passions become exacerbated; they grow argumentative; they have quarrels, difficulties, entanglements, abrupt and violent detachments. And they like it—they come back for more." [17]

This was certainly true. Some people—and Eastman claimed to be one—attended only once or twice. But it was much more common to return many times, to make the salon a regular part of one's social life. From the winter of 1912-13 and on into the following spring, evenings were held once, twice, sometimes three times a week. Usually, a discussion topic was announced in advance, and often special experts were invited to attend, but sometimes the conversation was confused, anarchic and, to some rigorous-minded participants, rather dismaying. Yet complaints were the exception. It was always stimulating to be at Mabel Dodge's because, as one newspaper reporter put it, she "seemed to know everybody worth knowing, not in the society way, but in the real way, and to get the right people together." [18] This did not happen by chance. The energy which had gone into collecting antiques now went into collecting people. Mabel became a self-described "Species of Head Hunter." She wanted to know the "Heads of Movements, Heads of Newspapers, Heads of all kinds of groups of

ROBERT A. ROSENSTONE

people." Upon meeting such individuals, she immediately issued invitations to the salon, and each would arrive with a claque of followers. The only person she ever remembered refusing to attend was French philosopher Henri Bergson.

The normal crowd represented an impressive cross-section of Manhattan's cultural and political circles. People from uptown— socialites, successful actors, and newspaper editors—mingled with residents of the Village—unknown poets, sculptors, or radical activists. There were middle-aged Progressives like Hapgood, Steffens, U. S. Commissioner of Immigration Frederic C. Howe, and Amos Pinchot, the well-known attorney and supporter of liberal causes. Leading a group of intellectuals, all recent graduates of Ivy League schools, was the brilliant, prematurely-wise Walter Lippmann, who two years after graduating from Harvard was already beginning to apply Freudian theories to political behavior. From the world of the visual arts came Marsden Hartley, Charles Demuth, Andrew Dasburg, John Marin, and Max Weber. Representing feminism was Henrietta Rodman, who had refused to take her husband's name and had successfully fought the Board of Education's rule that a married woman could not hold a teaching post. Also on hand was Margaret Sanger, an early proponent of both the joy of sex and the need for birth control. Radicals arrived in large numbers—Goldman and Berkman; anarchist Hippolyte Havel, who loudly denounced everyone as "goddamn bourgeois"; and Bill Haywood, head of the Industrial Workers of the World, who was living with a young schoolteacher in the Village.

Whether planned around a topic or merely free form, the evenings had a regular pattern. Gowned in silk or velvet, Mabel would stand near the door, give her hand to arriving guests, and murmur impersonal greetings. The front room would fill until all the chairs were taken, and people were sitting on the floor or lounging against the wall. It was a colorful crowd—"ladies in black velvet, wearing diamonds, ladies in batik and Greenwich village sacks, ladies with bobbed hair and mannish-cut garments, men in evening dress, men in workmen's clothes." [19] Sometimes there was a master of ceremonies—Stef, Hutch, or Lippmann—whose job it was to keep order. This was almost impossible. People might jump up, have their say, interrupt one another, grow angry or sarcastic, and, on occasion, storm out of the room. The talk could be brilliant or unintelligible, sober or riotous, but always it was charged with energy. Van Vechten remembered: "Arguments and discussion,

MABEL DODGE

floated in the air, were caught and twisted and hauled and tied, until the white salon itself was no longer static. There were undercurrents of emotion and sex."[20] No matter how fascinating the discussion, there was a break at midnight. The doors to the dining room were thrown open, and the crowd rushed in for a supper of Virginia ham, turkey, imported cheese and salads. The bar was well-stocked with rare scotch, wine, and liqueurs. Talk would continue as people mingled informally, and then the crowd would slowly drift away. Sometimes Mabel showed guests out, but it was not unknown for her to withdraw from the room long before the evening ended.

Subjects of discussion covered the full range of fashionable, artistic, and intellectual interests. There were political evenings, when Lippmann or Steffens expounded on government, Socialist leaders explained the doctrines of Marx, or others compared anarchism with syndicalism. Sex was a common topic; although to Mabel's dismay there was little talk of love, much was made of the need for healthy "sex expression". Abstract art was another favorite, possibly because it seemed difficult for many people to accept the new notion that painting and sculpture did not have to represent anything other than itself. Other occasions were devoted to eugenics, feminism, birth control, primitive cultures, poverty, newspapers and magazines, or foreign issues like the growing revolutionary war in Mexico.

Neither the topic nor the guest list could ensure success. This was a haphazard matter, the result of some strange alchemy, a subtle blend of people, subject and liquor intake that nobody could predict in advance. A much-anticipated poetry reading was ruined by two factors: the most eminent author present, Edwin Arlington Robinson "sat like a bump on a log and didn't express a thing," and then, when George Sylvester Vierick began to read his verse, the hefty Amy Lowell rose and sailed out "like a well-freighted frigate."[21] Several guests also departed hastily on the psychoanalytic evening, when A. A. Brill—one of the first American disciples of Freud—explained the nature of the unconscious and tried to show how it affected everyday behavior. Yet others judged this one of the most successful of occasions and demanded that more evenings be devoted to the same subject. Steffens claimed that at the salon he first heard of the "new psychology of Freud and Jung," and what was true for this sophisticated writer was no doubt so for many others as well.[22]

ROBERT A. ROSENSTONE

Sometimes a guest could be brilliant on one occasion and inarticulate on another. This was the case with Bill Haywood, one of the stars of the salon. Haywood was considered a dangerous man by many Americans, and the IWW—with its bindle-stiffs, tramp poet organizers, and calls for direct action—was the most feared of all radical organizations. Haywood was every inch the radical hero—a massive, slouchy, battered-looking, one-eyed man with a voice that could crackle with revolutionary sentiments. When he entered the salon it was, Van Vechten wrote, as if a "tremendous presence. . . filled the room. . . Debutantes knelt on the floor beside him, while he talked simply, but with an enthralling intensity. . . reinforcing his points by crushing the heels of his huge boots into the Shirvan rug or digging his great hands into the mauve tapestry, with which the divan was upholstered."[23]

Despite his usual eloquence, Haywood was a total failure on an evening devoted to what Mabel liked to call "Dangerous Characters". Anarchists, Socialists, and Wobblies were to give their views on direct action and sabotage. To ensure no interference from the police, Mabel shifted the normal meeting night, issued special invitations, and dramatically had the apartment doors bolted. She need not have bothered. Haywood "talked as though he were wading blindfolded in sand," and when Walter Lippmann attempted to draw him out with leading questions, his "lid drooped over his blind eye, and his heavy cheeks sagged lower," but nothing worth hearing issued from his mouth. Emma Goldman then took the floor. Sounding "like a severe schoolteacher in a scolding mood," she too rambled and never made an effective point. After her came Socialist William English Walling, who was no better than "smiling and bland".[24] But this was only to be expected. For Mabel and her friends, Socialists were too tame; like good bourgeois, they believed in electoral politics.

Haywood was much better when he told an audience that included Hartley, Dasburg, Marin and Francis Picabia that artists "thought themselves too special and separate" and spoke of a future when everybody would have enough leisure time to produce works of art. Mabel's old friend Janet Scudder, who had spent many painful years training in Paris, rose to her feet and scornfully said: "Do you realize that it takes twenty years to make an artist?" That began the battle. Haywood eloquently replied, Dasburg grew "flashing and witty", and soon people were passionately interrupting one another until "the air was vibrant with intellectual excitement and electrical with the appearance of new ideas and dawning changes." It was one of those times when, Mabel remembered, "We really had General Conversation."[25]

A different group of artists provided another rousing session. The ostensible topic was magazines. Mabel had invited the editors of the slick, popular *Metropolitan Magazine* to meet with the staff of the radical subculture's favorite journal, *The Masses*, an irreverent monthly whose contributing editors included John Sloan, George Bellows, and Art Young. What was supposed to have been a general discussion of ideas and policies degenerated into a confrontation, as the poor young men of *The Masses* denounced their commercially-minded counterparts. Young Maurice Becker shook his finger at *Metropolitan* art editor Will Bradley, referred to the *Metropolitan* as "a prostitute", and shouted, "How we loathe ourselves for selling drawings to go inside your covers."[26]

Such rude confrontation was hardly the rule. Witty and eloquent disagreements were more common, and one young man expressed the general attitude by writing, "Everyone was sophisticated to a frightening degree, and the smart repartee was battledored and shuttlecocked across that candle-lit room so rapidly that a youngster like myself could not keep pace with it."[27] Once an attempt was made to capture this repartee on paper. Hapgood had been asked to speak on what Mabel called "Sex Antagonism", that war between man and woman that she so well understood, and a stenographer was hired to record the conversation. But Hutch was a little drunk when he rose to speak, and the stenographer was not used to his vocabulary or odd juxtapositions. The resulting transcript was a disjointed jumble of ideas about sex, men, women, Wobblies, revolution, love, art, democracy, and anarchism that lurched between sharp insights and total nonsense. On reading it over, Steffens commented that it sounded much like the writing of Gertrude Stein.

However witty, entertaining, difficult, boring, or meaningless the conversation, by the spring of 1913, the salon was the most important thing in Mabel's life. Because of it, she was asked to contribute to magazines, serve on public boards and political committees, lend her name, money and organizing abilities to worthy causes. Yet all the whirl of activity did not make her life complete. Often the evenings left her feeling sad and painfully aware of the fact that she always slept alone. It is true that friends like Steffens, Lippmann, Hapgood, and Van Vechten were as attentive

ROBERT A. ROSENSTONE

as lovers—only none of these relationships was ever sealed in the flesh, and Mabel was a woman for whom the spiritual and the sexual went together. A brief and unsuccessful affair that spring showed that Mabel was ready for a more serious distraction to arise from the transcendant realm of love.

His name was John Reed. He was twenty-five, a graduate of Harvard in the 1910 class that produced Lippmann and T. S. Eliot, a contributing editor of *The Masses*, and a writer who had already achieved a considerable reputation among both uptown journalists and the residents of Greenwich Village. His short stories were spare slices of life that dealt with the underside of the big city—with bums, scrub women, prostitutes, con men, and cops—in a vision that blended shock with love, much like the realistic paintings of the Ash Can School. One of his poems had won an "honorable mention" in the first year (1912) of Harriet Monroe's new publication, *Poetry*, which carried works by William Butler Yeats, Ezra Pound, Amy Lowell, Vachel Lindsay, and William Carlos Williams. His father, a militant Progressive in Oregon politics, was close to Lincoln Steffens, who had been guiding young Reed's career and helping him to enter the world of New York journalism.

What distinguished Reed from many similar young men was not just an ability with words, but a propensity toward action. At prep school and Harvard, he frequently had been in trouble with authorities and after graduation, while classmates had sailed in luxury for a grand tour of the continent, Reed had worked across the Atlantic on a cattle boat and tramped alone through England, France, and Spain before settling in a hotel room on the Left Bank. His long poem, "A Day in Bohemia", had captured the new life style of the Village—"We dare to think as uptown wouldn't dare"—but he was hardly a typical Villager. Reed preferred hanging out in working-class bars, mingling with immigrants on the Lower East Side and talking with the girls of Satan's circus to attending literary meetings where people "Talk about talking and think about thinking, and swallow each other without even blinking."[28] No doubt it was this attitude which had kept him from going to Mabel's salon.

It almost seems inevitable that Mabel would fall in love with Reed. He was an incarnation of all the radical impulses of art and social change thrusting through Greenwich Village and being expressed at the salon. Only her account of their meeting is available; and however problematic the details, the emotional tenor rings true. The place was a crowded village apartment; the time, April 1913; the occasion, a talk by Bill Haywood on a silk strike that the IWW was supporting in Paterson, New Jersey. It was an old story. City officials and mill owners were working together. Police were clubbing and jailing strikers in large numbers, and the New York press was not reporting these events. Mabel claims to be the one who first suggested that, to receive proper news coverage, the strike should be brought to New York and re-enacted on the stage of Madison Square Garden. At this point Reed popped out of the crowd: "That's a *great* idea. . . we'll make a pageant of the strike! The first in the world!" She noticed he was big and full-chested, with glowing, olive green eyes, a high forehead set off by light brown curls "and two spots of light shining on his temples. . . his chin was the best of his face, for it had a beautiful swinging curve forward— the real poet's jawbone, strong and delicate above his round throat."[29]

Soon they were seeing a lot of each other. Reed went off to Paterson, was arrested, spent four days in jail with Wobbly prisoners, and emerged bursting with a radical excitement that suffused "War in Paterson", a piece for *The Masses*. This was the first step on a road that would run through the Mexican Revolution to Petrograd in 1917, where he would witness the Bolshevik Revolution, come home to write the classic *Ten Days That Shook the World*, help found the Communist Labor Party, return to Russia, and die there of typhus in 1920. The drive that would take him so far was already showing, and Mabel was captivated by his energy, passion, and ability to get things done. Together they were on the planning committee for the Paterson pageant. Reed wrote the scenario, persuaded Harvard classmate Bobby Jones to design the setting, and John Sloan to paint the scenery. He also led Villagers to Sunday meetings in Paterson to express solidarity with the silk workers, and he took charge of drilling masses of strikers for their on-stage roles.

The salon continued to meet, but Mabel was no longer always present. As with the Armory show, Mabel sensed the pageant was hers: "I knew I was enabling Reed to do what he was doing. I knew he couldn't have done it without me. I felt that I was behind him, pouring all the power in the universe through myself into him."[30] The performance took place on June 7 before a packed, raucous crowd in the Garden. It was such a success that some newspapers

ROBERT A. ROSENSTONE

hailed the birth of "a new art form", and many Bohemians had momentary visions of a revolutionary, popular theater with the power to engage the emotions of the masses. Yet this kind of elation was temporary. Partly intended to raise money, the pageant produced a deficit, and whatever publicity it brought proved unavailing—in August, the strike ended in complete defeat for the IWW. Neither of these facts bothered Mabel very much. When the financial report was released late in June, she and Reed were in Europe, and temporarily the salon was at an end.

It was a summer devoted to love, and for a short period, Mabel was ecstatic. Sex meant total surrender, yet Reed was a worthy lover who led her to say, "At last I learned what a honeymoon should be." Night after night at the Villa Curonia, he climbed into her bed, and the world vanished: "Nothing counted for me but. . .to lie close to him and empty myself over and over, flesh against flesh."[31] Such passion could not prevent problems from arising in the daylight. Mabel wanted to be the absolute center of his existence, but Reed was also interested in the old towns of Tuscany, the palaces, cathedrals, art works, and history that had once captivated Mabel. Now she grew jealous: "I hated to see him interested in things. I. . . didn't like to have him even *look* at churches and leave me out of his attention."[32]

The evenings recommenced when Mabel and Jack returned to New York in the fall of 1913, and he moved into 23 Fifth Avenue. Outwardly everything was the same as before, with similar crowds, topics, and a certain amount of press notoriety. But for her, the salon would never regain its former importance. She was caught in the grips of a power struggle, and Reed, who was half-boy, half-man, seemed impossible either to release or subdue. For Mabel, the evenings became a kind of battleground. She invited people in the hope that "When my value appeared greater to others, it would appear so to him and would make him want to be with me all the day."[33] But Reed was too committed to art, radical movements, and journalism to spend all his time with her. Mabel was driven into a frenzy at the sight of women approaching him, but she was equally jealous of the time he spent at *The Masses* office and other Village hangouts. By late fall, the relationship had degenerated into arguments, tears, quarrels, and recriminations that led to Mabel's swallowing an overdose of veronal. When she recovered, Jack fled the city, taking an assignment to cover the revolution of Pancho Villa in northern Mexico.

MABEL DODGE

148

In the four months that Reed was away, Mabel struggled to regain her equilibrium—this, after all, was the first time that a man had eluded her control. When she had briefly followed Jack to El Paso, Steffens had attempted to keep the salon going by hosting an evening devoted to British Labor Party visitors. But without Mabel, it was not the same, and he cancelled further meetings until her return. She started them again, but nothing could keep her mind off Reed. Finally the Wobblies were able to provide a meaningful diversion. Early in 1914, a young man who had attended the salon was arrested for leading groups of unemployed, homeless men and women into churches and synagogues to find shelter on cold winter nights. Mabel attended the trial and hosted meetings of support. These were crashed by the press, leading to headlines like "I.W.W. Throng Are Guests of Society Folk of Fifth Avenue", "Women in Evening Gowns Entertain Bill Haywood", "Agitators and the Unemployed in Home of Mrs. Mabel Dodge." As if this odd juxtaposition of social types were not newsworthy enough, each story solemnly reported that many of the women were engaged in the shocking practice of "smoking cigarettes."

Reed returned a full-fledged hero in April. He had braved gunfire while riding with the troops of Pancho Villa, and his active, colorful articles in the *Metropolitan* had made him famous. This was not good news for Mabel. At a "Reed in Mexico" evening she regarded him critically "and wondered why he looked so puffed up, as though he had been inflated by a pump. His chest swelled up under his chin, and he had to compress it to get the air into his lungs."[34] Two weeks later, he was off again, this time to investigate a massacre of coal strikers by militia at Ludlow, Colorado. Now Mabel had to understand she was losing him. They would spend a few weeks in Provincetown in June, then some time together in Italy, France, and England the next autumn, where Reed would be covering stories on the Western Front. But all this was dénouement. She, who was so attuned to the inner life of the psyche, was losing her lover to the external world of men and events, to armies, strikes, war, and revolution.

Not only was the affair with Reed drawing to an end, but so was the salon. The war would eventually shatter the fragile bond connecting art and politics, and in the postwar era, social and artistic experimentation would dwell in two separate realms. But even before the guns of August began to sound, Mabel was retreating from the daily issues of the world. Reed had come to

ROBERT A. ROSENSTONE

symbolize them all, and the loss of his love entailed the death of feelings and interests which had occupied her for two years. The spirit of the universe was moving in a new direction. Mabel was saying goodbye "to the gay, bombastic, and lovable boy with his shining brow; to the Labor Movement, the Revolution, and to anarchy. To the hope of subtly undermining the community with Hutch; and to all the illusions of being a power in the environment. My young lover was gone, and, it seemed, gone with him were the younger hopes of change. . ."[35]

Short-lived as it was, Mabel Dodge's salon has cast a long shadow in American cultural history. Memoirs of the period refer to the evenings in the most laudatory and ecstatic terms; yet it is difficult, perhaps impossible, to measure their impact upon the lives of active and creative men and women. For Mabel, the salon was a kind of unique spiritual and cultural oasis in the materialistic desert of American life. There is both truth and exaggeration in such a judgment. Enough other such centers did exist to show that the salon was only one outlet for the widespread social and cultural ferment of the prewar years.

Clearly, to attend the evenings was a splendid experience. Often they reflected the excitement of a subculture suddenly making connections between disparate schools of thought, social doctrines, movements in the arts. It was a youthful moment when people seemed in control of their destinies, when change seemed imminent, and when there was no conflict between reshaping the social order or oneself. At least this was the middle-class view, that of people who later had the time and inclination to write about themselves. Obviously part of the fascination was what has more recently been labelled "radical chic", the chance for those with sheltered lives to confront what seemed the brute reality and potential violence of class struggle and industrial warfare symbolized by anarchists and Wobblies. What it meant to those radicals who are silent witnesses of history is less apparent. Perhaps it was a rare chance to meet the oppressors face to face, to indulge in flirtations with class enemies, or merely to enjoy a warm evening of expensive food and drink.

Out of the salon and the Greenwich Village subculture that it represented, men and women carried a variety of beliefs into action. Lippmann went on to a lengthy career as one of America's premier political analysts; Sanger mothered the modern movement of birth control; Steffens resurfaced in the thirties as the guru of the Left with the publication of his *Autobiography*; artists such as Hartley, Dasburg, and Marin and poets such as Lowell attained secure places in American cultural history. These children of the middle class ultimately stayed within the bounds of respectability, but others could not. Reed was enshrined as a permanent radical hero by dying for the Russian Revolution. Many other radicals suffered from wartime hysteria. Haywood stood trial with 200 leading Wobblies who were unjustly convicted of sedition, then jumped bail, and fled to the Soviet Union, where he died in obscurity. Emma Goldman and Alexander Berkman were deported after the Red Scare raids of 1920 and remained exiles for the rest of their lives.

Mabel Dodge would outlive most of her regular guests, not dying until 1961. In 1915, she withdrew from Manhattan to a country estate in Croton, on the Hudson River. Then a few years later, she moved to New Mexico. She married twice more, first to artist Maurice Sterne, then to Tony Luhan, an Indian. In Taos, she helped to create an art colony, where for a time, she captured D. H. Lawrence. She travelled, was psychoanalyzed, and wrote voluminous memoirs, but never again was she at the center of an active world where great changes seemed possible. Only for two years had the spirit of the universe led Mabel Dodge to dwell amidst what she later called the "movers and shakers" of history.

NOTES

1. Margaret Sanger, *An Autobiography* (New York: Norton, 1938), 72-73; *The Autobiography of Lincoln Steffens* (New York: Harcourt, Brace, 1931), 655; Max Eastman, *Enjoyment of Living* (New York: Harper, 1948), 523.
2. Henry F. May, *The End of American Innocence* (New York: Knopf, 1959).
3. Mabel Dodge, *Intimate Memories—Background* (New York: Harcourt, Brace, 1933), 25-26. Dodge's four volumes of memoires are the best introduction to her life. The only biography, Emily Hahn, *Mabel: A Biography of Mabel Dodge Luhan* (Boston: Houghton Mifflin, 1977) is chatty, uncritical and full of factual mistakes.
4. Dodge, *Movers and Shakers*, 228.
5. Dodge, *Intimate Memories—European Experiences* (New York: Harcourt, Brace, 1935), 77.
6. Ibid., 453.
7. Quoted in Dodge, *Intimate Memories—Movers and Shakers* (New York: Harcourt, Brace, 1936), 27.
8. Quoted in ibid., 37.
9. Ibid., 36.

ROBERT A. ROSENSTONE

10. Letter to Stein in Donald Gallup, ed., *The Flowers of Friendship: Letters Written to Gertrude Stein* (New York: Knopf), 1953, 70-71.
11. "A Layman's View of the Art Exhibition," *The Outlook*, 103 (March 29, 1913), 719.
12. New York *Times* (March 16, 1913), 4, p. 6.
13. Dodge, *Movers and Shakers*, 47.
14. Ibid., 58.
15. Ibid., 80.
16. Ibid., 80-81.
17. Eastman, *Enjoyment of Living*, 523.
18. Quoted in Dodge, *Movers and Shakers*, 82.
19. Carl Van Vechten, *Peter Whiffle* (New York: Knopf, 1922), 134.
20. Ibid., 124.
21. Dodge, *Movers and Shakers*, 91.
22. Steffens, *Autobiography*, 655.
23. Van Vechten, *Peter Whiffle*, 125-126.
24. Dodge, *Movers and Shakers*, 89.
25. Ibid., 91.
26. Ibid., 87.
27. Charles H. Towne, *This New York of Mine* (New York: Cosmopolitan, 1931), 177-78.
28. John Reed, *The Day in Bohemia, or Life Among the Artists* (New York: printed for the author, 1913). For a full account of Reed's background see Robert A. Rosenstone, *Romantic Revolutionary: A Biography of John Reed* (New York: Knopf, 1975).
29. Dodge, *Movers and Shakers*, 189.
30. Ibid., 205.
31. Ibid., 215-16.
32. Ibid., 217-18.
33. Ibid., 234.
34. Ibid., 257
35. Ibid., 303.

MABEL DODGE

SALKA VIERTEL

Sundays in Mabery Road

Bruce Cook

It was a house at the foot of Santa Monica Canyon, only a few steps from the beach. To the west lay the Pacific, that vast Eastern ocean, which probably made this point seem to any European a kind of ultima Thule, the absolute end of the line.

That, at any rate, must have been what it meant to Salka Viertel: she had gone about as far as she could go. Born in Galicia late in the last century, when that piece of Poland was still attached to the Hapsburg Empire, she had made her way to Vienna at her earliest opportunity to pursue a career on the stage. There, after an apprenticeship that had taken her as far afield as Berlin and Max Reinhardt's *Deutsches Theater*, she was established as a leading actress with the *Neue Wiener Bühne* when she met a young director, who was also a poet, named Berthold Viertel. World War I was in its third year. He was on leave from the front, married, and with no apparent resources except his own overweening self-confidence. Yet he swore when he first came to know Salka that they would soon be married. And before the war was ended, he kept that promise. Their alliance proved for a time to be one of the firmest professional partnerships in the German theater; and it was to the very end one of the most engaging. Immediately after the war the two settled in Berlin, where, it seems, they worked with or came to know nearly everyone involved in the Berlin theater world of the twenties—among them, playwrights Brecht, Bronnen, Kaiser, Zuckmayer, and players Kortner, Homolka, Granach, and Lorre.

And somehow, between their involvement as founders of an avant-garde theater company, *Die Truppe*, and Berthold's additional work with F. W. Murnau in films, the busy couple even managed to bring three sons—Hans, Peter and Thomas—into the world.

The association with Murnau was what brought them, together with their children, all the way across an ocean and a continent to come at last to a halt on that farthest shore. In 1928, Berthold Viertel was invited to Hollywood to write the screenplay for F. W. Murnau's second American film, *The Four Devils*. He had every intention of staying on to direct films of his own, and so the whole family came along. Once Salka set eyes upon the Pacific, she knew that she had reached her destination, a kind of goal. "Everything was so lovely and peaceful," she remembers in her autobiography, *The Kindness of Strangers*, "the people on the pier and the merry-go-round and the swaying boats. I begged Berthold to let us live in Santa Monica." She had that passion for the beach and broad ocean that perhaps only a land-locked middle-European could generate. Her husband, for one, could not. Yet to satisfy her, he consented, and eventually Salka got her house by the ocean.

The address of the place she chose was 165 Mabery Road, and it was not at all grand by Hollywood standards. It became quite well known, however, among a certain select, though ever-growing, contingent of residents, emigrés, and visitors. In the beginning, their guests were newcomers, like themselves, who had come from Europe—people like Fred Zinnemann, the young Viennese film editor and soon-to-be director, and William Dieterle, the director whom the Viertels had known as an actor in Max Reinhardt's company. Or, if not European, then they were those, like Paul Muni, who had something of Europe about them: he had come from New York's Yiddish theater to star in Berthold's second Hollywood film as a director, *The Seven Faces*.

What established Salka most firmly as a hostess, however, was her friendship with Greta Garbo. That began at a party given by Ernst Lubitsch. Upon meeting, the two women hit it off marvelously well, and Garbo, it turned out, lived quite near the Viertels. She began dropping by very early in the morning, and the two would take long walks together along the beach. On one of them Garbo asked Salka why she did not write. While Salka might have answered that the reason was, of course, because she was an actress, she knew that she had not worked in that capacity since coming to Hollywood from Germany. And here was Garbo—*Garbo!*—asking Salka to

BRUCE COOK

write something suitable for her. Who could decline such an opportunity? Teamed with another woman of like interest, one whose command of English was much surer than Salka's, she produced the screen story, *Queen Christina*, which, on Garbo's say-so, was promptly bought by Metro-Goldwyn-Mayer. She was put on the payroll to work on the script.

Thus began Salka's career as a "Garbo specialist." It seemed quite a blessing, for at just about that time Berthold's luck gave out in Hollywood, and he returned to Berlin to look for film work during the period when the country was teetering on the brink of nazism. This new source of income enabled her to stay on in Santa Monica with their three sons until he could return. In the final reckoning, however, although it meant a decade of full-time employment for her, hitching her wagon to a star would prove somewhat risky.

As the crisis deepened in Germany, Salka became increasingly anxious for her husband's safety. He was under contract to a German film company and writing a screenplay when Hitler came to power. Boldly, perhaps even foolishly, Berthold Viertel, a Jew and an outspoken enemy of the Nazis, stayed on to finish the job. Only with the burning of the Reichstag did he and so many others—Thomas and Heinrich Mann, Bertold Brecht, Ernst Toller, Kurt Weill, Alfred Döblin, and Anna Seghers among them—give in at last and depart. Salka was expecting him to return to his family in Santa Monica, but instead he went off to London on the promise of a directing assignment from Alexander Korda.

The name of the picture was *Little Friend*, and with it Berthold Viertel took his place in English literature—not a very prominent place, to be sure. Say, one that is high up in one corner of the gallery in a seat beside Gerald Hamilton, who was the original for Christopher Isherwood's Mr. Norris. Berthold himself became raw material for Isherwood, who was his screenwriter on the production; and as Friedrich Bergmann in the rather short novel, *Prater Violet*, Berthold made his own quite indelible impression on readers. Here is how he is described by Isherwood at their first meeting:

> . . . .Bergmann jerked to his feet with startling suddenness, like Punch in a show. "A tragic Punch," I said to myself. I couldn't help smiling as we shook hands, because our introduction seemed so superfluous. There are meetings which are more like recognitions—this was one of them. Of course we know each other. The name, the voice, the

> features were inessential, I knew that face. It was the face of a political
> situation, an epoch. The face of Central Europe.

No doubt that was the face that Berthold Viertel presented to the world, brooding and explosive, for in the weeks of wide-ranging conversations that followed that first meeting the two talked at length of Berlin (which, of course, they had in common), of Hitler and his Nazis, and of the Reichstag trial which proceeded day by day even as they met and discussed the script of *Little Friend*. There was probably not a better companion for Berthold in all of England during those dark days than Isherwood.

He also talked about his family back in California—of Salka and his sons, and of their life there. As Isherwood recalled in his factual treatment of this episode in his third-person autobiography, *Christopher and His Kind*:

> Viertel described their white house with its green roof, standing amidst the subtropical vegetation of Santa Monica Canyon, three minutes from the Pacific Ocean. 165 Mabery Road—the British-sounding address became wildly exotic when Christopher tried to relate it to his idea of a canyon, a gigantic romantic ravine. He began to yearn to see this place; Viertel took it for granted that he would be visiting them there before long.

Eventually he did. Five years later when Isherwood emigrated to America, he made for Los Angeles and settled—where else?—in the Santa Monica Canyon. (Once, when I had occasion to visit him in his home, he stood at a window looking down upon the canyon and remarked that he had lived in five different places in America and they were all within sight at that moment.)

Aldous Huxley preceded Isherwood to America by two years and the returning Berthold Viertel by one. In the beginning Huxley had come for no more than an extended tour, expecting to stay about a year. However, having seen something of the American West and having renewed his friendship with that knockabout mystic, Gerald Heard, he decided in Los Angeles to stay on somewhat longer. The news from Europe, after all, was getting worse by the day! To make it easier for the Huxleys to remain, Anita Loos (the brunette who wrote *Gentlemen Prefer Blondes*) whom they had met years before in New York, offered to see what she could do about getting him a film writing job at M-G-M. This was 1938. Salka Viertel was now a veteran screenwriter there and especially well thought of because

157

of her proven ability to create roles for Greta Garbo (*Queen Christina* and *Conquest* had both originated with her). Salka's latest project for the actress was a story built around the role of Madame Curie, the Polish woman who, with her husband Pierre, discovered radium. She had read the biography of the scientist and suggested it to Garbo who was most enthusiastic. Anita Loos knew all about this, and also knowing that Salka always worked with a second writer, she brought her together with Huxley one evening in her home. Perhaps a collaboration on the Madame Curie story?

That was just about how it was managed. George Cukor was to be the director. The writing team turned out a "treatment" that satisfied them both but seemed to the M-G-M producer involved excessively "scientific." Through the next two years the screenplay of *Madame Curie* went through successive—and, no doubt, excessive—rewrites (even F. Scott Fitzgerald had a shot at it) in the course of which Greta Garbo lost interest in it. When the film was finally produced in 1941, it starred Greer Garson and Walter Pidgeon; and while it was not at all bad, it was certainly not the *scientific* epic that Huxley and Salka had envisioned. Their names, by the way, did not appear on the screen—nor, for that matter, did F. Scott Fitzgerald's: the last team to rewrite usually wins the prize. In fact, the picture would not be worth mentioning here, except that it brought Aldous Huxley and Salka Viertel together, and while their professional association lasted only eight weeks, they remained friends until Huxley's death. When he and his wife, Maria, at last admitted to themselves that they would be living in Los Angeles for quite some time, they bought a house in Pacific Palisades, just north of Salka's place. They were frequent guests at dinner and regular attendants when, during the war, she began her regular Sundays.

Both Huxley and Isherwood chose to remain in America because of the war. Both were committed pacifists by the time they arrived—Isherwood, in fact, put in time at a Quaker work camp when the United States did at last declare hostilities. It was because of Hitler and the war, too, that Hollywood's German colony began to grow so astonishingly—not just in quantity, but in variety, as well. There had always been movie people. Beginning with Erich von Stroheim, German and Austrian directors and actors had begun to find their way over during the silent era when the language barrier seemed not quite so formidable—and the Viertels, of course, were among them. But with Hitler's seizure of power in 1934, the trickle became a steady stream, one that brought to America such considerable talents as Fritz Lang, Billy Wilder, Oscar Homolka, and Luise Rainer. Then, with the coming of the war, the stream became a river on which were borne not just movie people, but also playwrights, novelists, composers, and philosophers. And if that river did not exactly bring a new intellectual flowering to the sandy soil surrounding Los Angeles, neither did it evaporate there in the desert. The situation was such that by 1941 Aldous Huxley could remark casually of his new neighbors in a letter, "We were polite to the Feuchtwangers, and the Manns live exactly opposite so we meet on our walks."

"The Manns," in this case, were the Thomas Manns. They had moved only recently to Pacific Palisades, having come there by stages from Zurich and Princeton. Mann, by far the brightest star in the émigré constellation, had come only with misgivings to California; although once settled, he liked it well enough and found no trouble whatever in writing there. But his wife Katja never came to terms with their new home (the Manns were among the first of the intellectual refugees to take out citizenship papers). Maria Huxley, again in a letter, described them at a dinner: "He was peaceful and pacifying; she was hating and violent and we would not discuss it; besides—to be rude about America while you *have* to remain in it."

Heinrich Mann, his brother, was also there, a late arrival from France. Both he and Lion Feuchtwanger had been in Paris at the time of the fall of France. Mann effected an immediate escape over the Pyrenees to Spain and out by way of Portugal. Feuchtwanger made it to the south of France where he was interned for a year by the Vichy government before he, too, managed an exit by the same route. Feuchtwanger, Franz Werfel, and Thomas Mann were about the only émigré novelists who were able to live on their book royalties once they had arrived in the United States. Others were in real financial difficulties during their entire stay, and had to depend upon secondary employment or the generosity of friends. To their everlasting credit, some of the motion picture studios arranged pro-forma jobs for a few writers, acting as employers-of-record to facilitate emigration. Alfred Döblin was taken on by M-G-M for a brief period; and Heinrich Mann, who at age sixty-nine knew little English, was hired by Warner Brothers as a screenwriter.

Relations were never easy between the brothers Mann. Heinrich, the elder, leaned much further to the Left, politically, than Thomas, who often seemed a very reluctant democrat; and sibling rivalries carrying, as they often do, into old age, it couldn't have helped matters at all that Heinrich's reputation as a novelist didn't really extend much beyond the German-speaking world whereas Thomas' novels and stories had been translated into virtually every European language. Finally, whether he knew it or not (for Thomas apparently tried to keep this secret from him), Heinrich came to be almost totally financially dependent upon his brother. At his age, that must have been hard to take.

Considering all this, it seemed a good idea to bring the two of them together to celebrate Heinrich's seventieth birthday—but though everyone agreed, it was not at all easy to arrange. On the date in question, Thomas Mann was to receive an honorary degree from the University of California at Berkeley; he was then scheduled to give a series of lectures there that would hold him at the university for many weeks more. So, some three months after Heinrich Mann's chronological birthday, a number of "German writers in exile," including both brothers, Bruno Frank, Alfred Döblin, Franz Werfel, Lion Feuchtwanger and Ludwig Marcuse, gathered with their wives to celebrate a ceremonial anniversary in his honor. Where? Where else but at Mabery Road? Salka Viertel was the hostess, of course. Berthold, although long returned from London, had been unable to find employment in Hollywood and had gone off to New York to look for work in the theater; on the appointed evening he sent a telegram welcoming them all and adding his congratulations. Alfred Döblin described the scene in a letter to another novelist, Hermann Kesten:

> . . . .When we recently celebrated Heinrich Mann's 70th birthday at Salka Viertel's, it was as it once had been: Thomas Mann drew out a manuscript and congratulated him from it. Then the brother pulled out his paper and read the thanks written on it as we sat at dessert—about 20 husbands and wives listened to German literature discussed. Feuchtwanger, Werfel, Mehring, the Reinhardts were there, as well as some from films. The war seemed a long way off.

Afterward, Salka remarked to novelist Bruno Frank how moved she had been by the mutual tributes read by the two brothers (even though Thomas Mann's had been so long it caused the roast to be served overdone).

"Yes," said Bruno Frank. "They write and read such ceremonial evaluations of each other every ten years."

Thomas Mann—aloof, rather cold, and keenly aware of his

position as the leading representative of *deutsche Kultur* outside Nazi Germany—frequently irritated and angered the other members of the émigré community: and his inherent conservatism frequently put him at odds with the rest. The Free Germany Committee, of which Mann was a member, met at the home of Salka Viertel in 1943 to hammer out a fairly restrained statement to the effect that the German people should not be thought of as the creators of the Nazi terror, but rather as its first victim. Mann participated in the drafting of the message, applying the brake as he usually did; and at last it was worked out, apparently to everyone's satisfaction. The next day, however, Mann called the other members of the Committee and asked that his name be removed from the statement. Why? Marthe Feuchtwanger has given it as her opinion that "Mann didn't want to be involved in something he considered pro-Communistic."

Most of the émigré community was upset with him. Bertolt Brecht was furious. He wrote him an angry letter, which Mann notes in his *Doktor Faustus* diary, *The Story of a Novel*: "One letter from Bert Brecht, taking me to task for my lack of faith in German democracy. In what way had I shown it, this lack of faith? And was the charge justified?" There had never been any love lost between the two men. To Mann, Brecht represented all that was pernicious in Weimar culture. When his daugher Erika passed on a book of the playwright's stories to her father, urging that he read it, he took it reluctantly and read a few of them; he returned the book with the comment, "So, the monster has talent!" The monster also had influence among their contemporaries; and Mann felt called upon to defend himself in a letter to him:

> . . . .Where will we be, if we have prematurely vouched for the victory of the better and higher impulses within Germany? Let her military defeat take place, let the hour ripen when the Germans themselves settle accounts with the villains with a thoroughness, a ruthlessness such as the world scarcely dares to hope for from our unrevolutionary people. That will be the moment for us on the outside to testify that Germany is free, that Germany has truly cleansed herself, that Germany must live.

Brecht was neither satisfied nor mollified by Mann's rhetoric. "It would not be an exaggeration to say that Brecht hated him," Marthe Feuchtwanger told me.

Yes, Bertolt Brecht was also there on the scene, a very

prominent "German writer in exile," though not one welcome at the *Mannfest*. A late arrival, he had crossed the entire length of the Soviet Union via the Trans-Siberian Railway to depart from Vladivostok only days before the German invasion of Russia on a Swedish freighter. He disembarked in San Pedro in the company of his wife, Helene Weigel, their two children, and his mistress, Ruth Berlau. Although they were met there by Marthe Feuchtwanger and that incomparable character actor, Alexander Granach, and driven off to their new home in Hollywood, it wasn't long until Brecht was in close and frequent contact with Salka Viertel. They had known one another since the twenties in Berlin. Berthold and Salka both liked him; and that in itself was significant, for he was in some ways not a likeable man: they were willing to go that extra distance that he seemed to require of everyone. Salka, in fact, made it possible for Brecht to solve the inevitable problem that arose with wife and mistress under the same roof. She offered to take in Ruth Berlau; she put her up in the apartment above her garage. When he was able to do so, Brecht bought a house in Santa Monica in order to be nearer her; and, when he did, he became a constant visitor there in Mabery Road.

He grew quite close to Salka. One night the three of them—she, Brecht, and Ruth Berlau—sat up late having what Brecht would later call a "refugee conversation." Salka, who had been able to get all her family out of Poland, confessed to them that she often felt guilty that she had been "spared." Brecht told her that he, too, had had these feelings; the next morning she found tucked under her door a poem that he had written:

> I know, naturally: only through luck
> Have I survived so many friends. But last night in a dream
> I heard these same friends say to me: "The strong survive."
> And I hated myself.

She knew that he understood.

Among those whom Salka had been able to bring out of Europe was her mother, who arrived, even later than Brecht, by the same route, travelling all the way across wartime Russia and Siberia and then across the Pacific. Her mother was able to bring with her not much more than the clothes on her back and her recipe for chocolate cake; and it is with those chocolate cakes she baked on Mabery Road that Bertolt Brecht is forever associated in the minds of some of those who knew him there at Salka's. The American movie comedy writer and director Mel Frank remembers that, as if by magic, Brecht would appear, with or without Berlau, whenever a cake was in the oven.

By the middle of the war, Salka Viertel's regular Sundays in Mabery Road had become perhaps the last great salon, one attended by Europe's exiled intellectual elite, as well as by some of Hollywood's most glamourous figures. But it should be evident that hers was a salon of a rather special sort—*heimisch, gemütlich, bequem*—one where chocolate cake was more likely to be eaten than canapes, one that perfectly suited the relaxed and generous style of the hostess. Yet she attracted Hollywood's serious people—the writers, the directors, the émigré novelists, the theater people just in from New York. Where did Christopher Isherwood at last meet Bertolt Brecht? At Salka's. Where was George Cukor a regular? At Salka's. Where was the first place Harold Clurman headed when he jumped off the 20th Century Limited? To Salka's. "I remember it," says Mel Frank, "as a complete striation, an incredible spectrum of Hollywood's most interesting people. You might meet Chaplin, Garbo, and Dietrich there—and only there!— as well as the in-people and the out-people, all the serious composers and writers in town, including, of course that whole émigré community. She was *very* good about bringing people together. She was very helpful that way."

How? She got jobs for a few, and arranged informal charity from rich movie patrons for the rest. She served as intermediary between Brecht and Berthold Viertel in the early stages of negotiations for a New York production of *The Private Life of the Master Race*. She had her own agent, Frederick Kohner, handle some of the more employable émigrés.

Of course, things did not always work out as she hoped. One of the first she had tried to help was the composer, Arnold Schoenberg, with whom her brother Edward had studied in Berlin years before. When Schoenberg arrived in Hollywood in the thirties, she suspected that he was in rather difficult circumstances; after making a few discreet inquiries, she went to him and offered to arrange a meeting between him and her boss at M-G-M, Irving Thalberg, about the possibility of scoring the film of *The Good Earth*, which was about to begin shooting. She told Schoenberg not to consider doing it unless he were willing to compromise; he agreed that he was ready to do that; and so she did as she had offered, and brought the two together. She was present at the meeting in Thalberg's office, and she listened dumbstruck as Schoenberg explained that of course he could not agree to work unless he were given complete control over the film. What did that entail? He would write the score *first*, of course; and then coach the actors and actresses in delivering their lines in the proper key and right rhythm. Clearly, what he had in mind was turning *The Good Earth* into a work for *Sprechstimme* on the order of his earlier *Pierrot Lunaire*. Thalberg, although truly impressed by Schoenberg, declined the opportunity the composer had given him to turn the movie into a "serious" work of art.

In spite of the fact that her reputation as a Hollywood hostess was made during the war years, they were very hard for Salka personally. There were general worries about the war; and there was the despair she felt for the many she had known in Vienna and Berlin and Poland who had not been able to get out. Her own life was emptier than ever before. The years of separation endured by Salka and Berthold had at last taken their final toll: the two were divorced in 1944.

The year before she had lost her screenwriting job at Metro-Goldwyn-Mayer. Of course the difficulty was Salka's role as the "Garbo specialist." She had worked on other things, but in the minds of the studio executives she was still the writer they had hired to turn out stories and scripts for Garbo; and, as the Swedish actress turned down project after project, and become more and more reclusive, Salka herself began to seem to them somewhat superfluous. The last thing she worked on for Garbo was *Song of Russia*. Like *Madame Curie*, it was turned down by the star and passed on to another actress: Jean Peters played it opposite Robert Taylor. They took their revenge on Garbo by firing Salka.

Thrown onto her own, she had no immediate choice but to try another Garbo project, this time for an independent producer in collaboration with a French screenwriter of Russian parentage, Vladimir Pozner. Garbo seemed behind them on this one. She dropped by Mabery Street frequently to read what the two had done and to offer encouragement. In the end, however, she was no more willing to go with this script than with any of the others that had been offered her at M-G-M. That ended Salka Viertel's professional association with Greta Garbo.

Brecht approached her, proposing that they collaborate on a screen story. "Why shouldn't we be able to do as well as any

Hollywood hack?" he wanted to know. Yet, as they met daily at Salka's to shape the story, she soon found that, although Brecht had always promoted team authorship, he certainly demanded to be captain of the team. At last, in desperation, she asked that they bring another writer in on the project, one who might serve as referee to their battles. Brecht was willing, and so Vladimir Pozner was welcomed aboard. The fights continued, however; by Pozner's own account, Brecht seems to have been just as autocratic as before. The playwright would lay down the law on a scene; Salka would demand an explanation, a motivation, a justification.

"Why?" she would ask. "I want to know why!"

"Because I said so," Brecht would shout. "That's enough!" Finally, as things calmed down, he would say something conciliatory. Once: "Above all, let us not for one moment forget that we are writing this scenario to sell it."

But they never did sell the story, which was called *Silent Witness* and was set in France just after liberation. By that late date, 1945, producers may have felt that the war was going out of style. In their own crude fashion, they were right, of course. The war was over in Europe, and would soon come to a sudden, startling end in the Pacific as well. With peace came the inevitable break-up of the émigré community in Hollywood. Even many of those who had taken out citizenship papers had no real intention of staying on; they were refugees now ready to return. Brecht and Heinrich Mann were courted by the culture commissars of the German Democratic Republic, and were welcomed back to East Germany. Thomas Mann remained in America until 1952, and then, dismayed at the rise of McCarthyism, returned to Europe and settled in Switzerland. A few stayed on—Herbert Marcuse, Lion Feuchtwanger, Arnold Schoenberg—but over the decade that followed the war there was a general reverse migration that brought many home to receive the honors and homage denied them during the Hitler years.

Eventually, Salka Viertel returned as well. Things grew increasingly difficult for her financially. She managed to stay more or less active as a screenwriter, and had two more of her scripts produced. But assignments were few and far between; and free-lance projects of the kind she engaged in with Brecht and Pozner were always risky. Finally, after decades in the house on Mabery Road, she said goodbye to it and to the ocean she loved, and left Los Angeles for good. After some passport difficulties—her associations with Brecht and others had left her with that curious label, "premature anti-Fascist"—she departed in 1953 for Klosters in Switzerland where she lived near her son, the novelist and screenwriter Peter Viertel. Years before, when she was not much more than a girl, a gypsy had told her that she would know her greatest happiness near water, and that had been so. Writing her autobiography, it seemed to her that the best part of her life had been spent there in Santa Monica—the Sundays and the dinner parties, the walks along the beach. There was no body of water of any considerable size near her there in Klosters. Only mountains. She died there in 1978.

SALKA VIERTEL

KAREL CAPEK

The Friday Group in Prague

Joseph Wechsberg

Every Friday after 1921, a brilliant gathering was held in Prague at the house of Karel Capek, novelist, essayist and playwright, who had been born, the son of a country doctor, on January 9, 1890, in the Bohemian village of Male Svatonovice. All his life he had suffered from a spinal disease, and, as an adolescent, he had begun writing to forget his pain. Later, he studied philosophy in Prague, Berlin and Paris, returning to Prague, and literature, in 1917. Sometimes he collaborated with his brother Josef, a painter who illustrated many of his books. Capek had vision and courage, and like Franz Kafka in Prague, he too saw the future, as only a poet can see it; but he also observed the smaller men around him, and paid attention to their problems. In English-speaking countries he is still best known for his visionary dramas, such as *R.U.R.*, in which he describes a robot that threatens mankind with extinction; the robot bears a certain resemblance to the legendary Golem, the figure of clay that comes alive when the High Rabbi puts the *shem*, a capsule containing the magic formula, into its mouth.

Capek wrote other visionary plays, among them *Krakatit, The War with the Newts,* and *The Absolute at Large*. By 1936, Hitler's tyranny had already started; and *The War with the Newts* is a thinly disguised allegory about the true nature of totalitarianism. At the same time, however, Capek was the recorder and biographer of Thomas Garrigue Masaryk, the great philosopher who became the founder and first President of Czechoslovakia. While Masaryk spoke—haltingly and reluctantly—Capek listened, and they produced *President Masaryk Tells His Story,* and *Masaryk on Thought and Life: Conversations with Karel Capek.* As a true "liberator," Masaryk always attempted to settle the crises between the Czechs and the Slovaks. He himself came from Moravia, and had studied in Vienna. When he met Capek, the two men understood one another, though nothing, or little, could be said.

"It is very difficult to tell the story of the *Patecnici* in a few pages," writes Dr. K. Scheinpflug, one of Capek's heirs. *Patek* in Czech means "Friday", and the members of the informal, but extremely well-informed group around Capek were the *Patecnici,* the "Friday men". "They were intellectuals, writers, literary critics, journalists, scientists, philosophers," and "they would meet in Capek's house every Friday at five p.m. for about two hours, talking about everything that interested them." In Prague it was often whispered that the Friday men were members of a conspiracy, that they were running the country; but that was nonsensical. Their meetings, which began in 1921, lasted until Capek's death late in 1938. Some "Friday men", friends of Capek, went there regularly, and others once in a while; some later dropped out and were replaced by others. Among the best known, certainly today in Prague, were V. Vancura, O. Fischer, J. Kopta, E. Bass, J. Palivec, K. Polacek, J. Kodicek, A. Hoffmeister, F. Langer, F. Kubka, J. Mahen, J. Mach, A. Fuchs, V. Mathesius, J. Mukarovsky, J. B. Kozak, J. Susta, V. Rabas, and V. Rada—a fine list of the best minds of a westernized nation. No similar group has ever existed elsewhere. Many wrote for *Lidove Noviny,* the finest newspaper in Prague between the wars.

I then lived in Prague, and occasionally wrote for *Lidove Noviny,* called *Kursivky,* the small feuilletons in italic letters that were Karel Capek's domain. But I was too young to know Capek and to join the *Patecnici.* Little has been written about them since then. In January 1965, the writer and literary critic Bohumil Prikryl talked in the City Library of Prague about the great days of Capek's Friday meetings. He had a difficult job. The *Patecnici* were seldom mentioned because it had been silently agreed to keep their conversations confidential; hence the legend of the "conspiracy". The most important member of the group was President Masaryk himself. It was an exclusive gathering; money and fame wouldn't help you to get in. But it was never a secret society.

The first Friday meetings took place in 1921, when Capek lived in

JOSEPH WECHSBERG

Ricni ulice, overlooking the Vltava (Moldau). In May 1925, he moved into a small double house in the Vinohrady district, with his brother Josef. The street has changed its name, as have so many others in Prague. Originally it was called V stromkach ("In the Trees"—which gives an idea of the location of the house); later, it became known as uzka ulice, "narrow street"; and, finally, it was named ulice bratri Capku, the "street of the Brothers Capek." In his new house Capek had space for about forty people. Chairs were arranged along the walls of the big downstairs room. Near the entrance was a small table and chair where Capek sat; and he himself would get up and open the door. Next to him two chairs were kept vacant for important people who might come from Prague or elsewhere. When the room was overcrowded some guests would sit in the next room; and the door was kept open. When Capek rebuilt the attic of his house, the Friday meetings were kept in the *mansarda*.

Most of us know an author only through his writing, not through meeting and observing him. The *Patecnici* knew each other. They were relaxed because, though they recognised that their ideas might differ, they were in sympathetic company. Capek himself would greet everybody, extending his small hand, saying *"Vitam, Vas,"* "Be welcome!" Basically, the *Patecnici* were Capek's friends from all walks of life; they included scientists, artists and politicians.

The arrangements were exceedingly simple. "One didn't go to Capek's house to eat or drink," a member of the gathering told me years after Capek's death. There would be black coffee, the life elixir of Continental intellectuals, and perhaps a glass of Bohemian wine or small glasses of *slivovitz*, which looks like water but is very strong plum brandy. The guests might also bring refreshments. Everybody was supposed to know what was going on at home and abroad; and lively arguments took place. Capek was *primus inter pares*; but he neither demanded nor was accorded special privileges.

He was nervous when expecting the guest of honour. The visit was never announced, but if the *Patecnici* saw a few red roses in a small vase on the small table, they knew that President Masaryk would sit next to Capek.

The President sometimes came by car, and sometimes walked all the way from Hradcany Castle, across the beautiful Charles Bridge. He would then cross Vaclavske Square and start the ascent to Vinohrady, named for the vineyards that originally covered these slopes. It was a long walk; and Masaryk, born in 1850, was then in his mid-seventies; but he was never tired. (Nor was he accompanied by any security men; he felt at ease among his people, which sounds incredible today.) He would enter and greet his fellow guests and look at his watch, to see how much time he could spare. Once he came early, before five o'clock. Meetings began about that time, and he asked if it were Friday. "Yes, Mr. President." "Good," he said, "I thought I was getting mixed up."

Sometimes the President would be accompanied by Edvard Benes, then his Minister of Foreign Affairs and later his successor. Benes was listened to respectfully, as the most travelled, best-informed and most experienced member of the group. Prikryl gives the impression that there was almost a father-son relationship between Masaryk and Benes, and also between Masaryk and Karel Capek, who was forty years younger. Benes sometimes spoke at great length—he seemed to live only for his work; whereas Masaryk said little, a few well-chosen words, maybe a sentence or two. In his books Capek has described Masaryk's slightly reluctant attitude. He often hesitated before speaking, and never made an unnecessary remark. Once he was asked about the role of Benes abroad, during the long fight for liberation; then Masaryk didn't hesitate: "Without Benes, we wouldn't have the Republic." On another occasion there was talk about an ambitious, even dangerous politician. His companions, having said what they thought, looked at the President. "Not a nice man," he said, and everybody felt it was enough.

One Friday they discussed the problem of the so-called 'Zelena Hora manuscript.' In 1817 a man named Vaclav Hanka declared that he had found a thirteenth-century manuscript, written in Czech, underneath the church-tower in the Bohemian town of Kralovy Dvur. Czech nationalists were overjoyed. This discovery proved that their nation had existed and spoken its own language six centuries ago. But, in 1886, Masaryk published in his magazine *Athenaeum* a critical essay, arguing that the manuscript was a forgery. Masaryk had just been appointed professor of philosophy at the Czech University in Prague; and the nationalists were furious. They knew he was right, but he need not have been so frank! Masaryk's motto, however, was the old motto of Jan Hus and King George of Podebrady, *Pravda Vitezi* - "Truth Prevails." At the end of the conversation about the manuscript, Masaryk turned to his old friend, Jan Herben. "It was rather fun, wasn't it? When they

JOSEPH WECHSBERG

said in the newspapers that we were traitors, and that they were going to expel us from the country." "Today that may seem funny, Mr. President," Herben answered gravely, "but it wasn't funny when it happened."

At the end of 1926, the Friday meeting fell on Sylvester, New Year's Eve. Masaryk was there again; and this time everyone stayed together through the end of the old year. At midnight, three actors dressed to look like the Three Wise Men came to wish them luck and sing a Christmas carol that Capek had written. Apparently it was an ironical, political song; the matter was reported and some anti-Masaryk newspapers sued for slander. A joke was a joke, they said, but not in the presence of the President of the Republic.

Perhaps Capek wanted a visible memory of the Friday meetings, for, one Friday in spring, he asked the *Patecnici* to come out into his garden. (Capek considered his garden a true cosmos, and there wrote of mankind in general without ever leaving it.) He had prepared a few birch twigs and several spades. Every *Patecnik*, including Masaryk and Benes, made a little hole and planted a twig, which today are flourishing trees. At another meeting, having become interested in photography, Capek took snapshots of all his guests.

When the conversation was lagging, Capek introduced a subject; and soon there was a genuine argument in progress. He often surprised his friends. He could talk with each man in his own personal language, and when three former members of the Czechoslovak Legion—the playwright Frantisek Langer, and the writers Josef Kopta and Bohumil Prikryl—reminisced and used Russian phrases, Capek nodded and spoke a few Russian words. He liked people who agreed with him; but he liked those who disagreed even better. They presented a challenge; he could try to make them change their minds. "He understood that the simple things are often complicated, and many complicated things are basically simple," a *Patecnik* remembers. "Without loving people, one cannot become a writer," Capek once said. Always interested in human dramas, he did his best to discover the whole truth. There was no such thing as a "half-truth," he said. But he had a healthy scepticism. He refused to agree that there was some magic formula, capable of opening every secret.

His readers felt his great sympathy for mankind, because they liked him personally, even those whom he had never met. They understood that he was one of them. He admired extraordinary

KAREL CAPEK

achievements, but also appreciated the most humble efforts. Capek was convinced that every human being should labour in his separate sphere. Once he was asked how he employed his leisure. "I work," he replied.

He was always an educationalist, even when, as in his feuilletons for *Lidove Noviny*, he entertained his readers. The list of his books is long. He wrote novels and books for children (which were very popular with adults); he was a reporter, translator, dramatic critic and producer of his own plays. He was at the same time a photographer, cartoonist, gardener and house-builder. As Masaryk's biographer, and the recorder of the President's thoughts, he made a permanent contribution to history.

"Every important man has enemies," a member of the group observed. Though the attacks of his enemies saddened him, Capek never complained, and he did not like to criticize others. It was rare for a new book written by a member to be criticized. The *Patecnici* revered his energy. Despite ill-health, he seemed to have time for everything. As president of the P.E.N. Club, he travelled all over Europe, and people from everywhere came to visit him. The friends called his house "Czechoslovakia's embassy for the whole world".

The members of the Friday group knew what it meant for Capek—indeed, for all of them—when Masaryk, who had resigned two years earlier, died in his country-house, Castle Lany, on September 14, 1937. Capek didn't talk about his friend's death, but, the following Friday, there was a small wreath on the chair Masaryk had occupied, with a small black band and a card inscribed "*Vzpominame*", "we remember." He himself died just over a year later, on December 25, 1938, and was thus spared witnessing the tragedy of his country's occupation. There were no more Friday meetings. Capek was quietly buried at Vysehrad ("The High Castle"), the Czech pantheon where the nation buries its great dead. There, too, are the graves of Smetana and Dvorak, the poets Josef Hora and Vitezslav Nezval, the sculptor Jan Myslbek, the painter Mikolas Ales, and many others. Some of the *Patecnici* went abroad to fight; others fought at home. Some died in German camps; some were executed. "And that," said Prikryl, one of the few survivors, in 1965, "is the story of the Fridays and the *Patecnici*, among them a certain Karel Capek, whom his nation considered a national artist." Meanwhile, Europe at large has learned to regard him as both a citizen and artist of the world.

JOSEPH WECHSBERG

LADY CUNARD

A Celebrated London Hostess

Harold Acton

Whenever I revisit the Wallace Collection my thoughts return spontaneously to Lady Cunard, and when, less often, I revisit the Soane Museum I think of Lady Colefax. These ladies were the two pre-eminent cosmopolitan hostesses in the London of the nineteen-twenties and thirties; and the difference between their personalities and ambience are evoked for me by these distinctive museums, the former spacious, the latter claustrophobic. Some have compared them to the Biblical Martha and Mary; but that is too superficial an analogy.

Among the Fragonards and the Louis Quinze furniture of Hertford House, especially when a musical clock tinkles the hour, I can visualize Lady Cunard stepping lightly towards me with a smile of greeting, as in her own drawing-room at 7 Grosvenor Square, though her exquisite fragrance has evaporated.

She was invariably later than her guests, most of whom were known to each other and could exchange desultory gossip while waiting, though here and there a stranger from the Continent might sit in silent embarrassment apart, as if he had mistaken the address. Unless one were an intimate, this pre-prandial interval without the hostess could be daunting, a *mauvais quart d'heure*. But the arrival of the hostess was like a burst of melody. The shy stranger would be introduced in a brief expository phrase: "he has just flown in from Finland. . . writing a biography of Sibelius. . ."

Lady Cunard delighted in mixing her guests like cocktails with unexpected ingredients. The gazelles were induced to sit beside the lions, who were either musical or literary; but there was also a sprinkling of heterogeneous professions. Sir Thomas Beecham and George Moore were the *Lares* and *Penates*; and one was likely to meet one or the other or both until 1933 when Moore died. Even then his shadow seemed to linger among the bibelots. For me the presence of either great novelist or musician added a glamour to the occasion: Sir Thomas, the godfather of opera in England, with his trim Valois beard and his fruity delivery, impeccably dressed; George Moore dishevelled by contrast as if he had risen from his cluttered writing desk, an old gentleman with a baby-pink complexion and aquamarine eyes which gazed as if he were seeing the world for the first time, white-haired and mustachio'd Adam in the garden of Eden, surprised by what he saw.

Such established lions could be intimidating to younger guests. Not that they scowled or growled. Sir Thomas often seemed distracted during dinner, absorbed in some operatic score, humming to himself or tapping the table, oblivious of the ladies on either side until our hostess called him to order with some question that required a prompt reply. He surveyed the assembly with a proprietory air, conscious that he held the master key to our hostess's heart. George Moore, addressed as G. M., was his privileged rival who had fallen in love with Lady Cunard before her marriage. He would have preferred a *tête-a-tête* with her and resented the intrusion of others—especially of Sir Thomas. Nobody has described him better than Max Beerbohm, who wrote: "Whatever was in his mind, no matter where he was nor what his audience, he said. And when he had nothing to say, he said nothing. Which of these courses in an average drawing-room needs the greater courage—to say simply anything, or to sit saying simply nothing? I think I used to rate Moore's silences his finer triumph. They were so unutterably blank. And yet, in some remote way, they so dominated the current chatter."

Lady Cunard's was not an average drawing-room, and she could make him talk with dramatic effect, about "some i-de-a that had lately been simmering in his brain." Having been introduced to him as a native of Florence who wrote like Aubrey Beardsley, he decided that I was the very person to translate his *Confessions of a Young Man* into Italian. "It would give me pleasure to hear it in the Tuscan tongue," he said, "and while translating my book you would learn to write good English." Of our mutual friend Jacques-Emile

HAROLD ACTON

Blanche, who had painted his portrait (and mine in early youth) he was unexpectedly scornful. "A mere society painter for the popular magazines," he pronounced, "and he fancies himself as a writer. He is not to be taken seriously. A wishy-washy *mondain*! When I think of Manet and Degas, and one should always think of them, Blanche is a miserable mock." It was useless to try and defend Blanche against his onslaught. I had dropped a brick; but it had roused his eloquence.

He had been voluble and gregarious in the Paris of his beloved Manet and in the Dublin of the Celtic Renaissance, but now he had retired to his hermitage in Ebury Street whence very few could tempt him, for he could not bear the sight of friends growing old, of Mrs. Charles Hunter, for instance, who had given him the Bible that was to inspire *The Brook Kerith*. But Lady Cunard was ageless. Had he not likened her to a sparkling fountain that ever renews itself? When I spoke to her about his charming dedication of *Ulick and Soracha* she feigned slight annoyance, fearing that it made her ridiculous. G. M. never minded being ridiculous: it was his *petit luxe* as he remarked. Sometimes his deliberate use of archaisms sounded grotesque: obviously he relished pronouncing them with emphasis, in impish revolt against "the flat, worn-out idiom that is written in the newspapers and spoken in drawing-rooms." He has faithfully recorded:[1] "So far as my small power permits me, I have striven hard to accustom the London drawing-room to the word *belly*, being convinced that there is no real morality in substituting *stomach* for *belly*: and invariably I interrupt her who speaks of her dog as a lady—Madam, I suppose you refer to your bitch. My authority is slight, but such as it is I have tried to use it. . . *Sick* means *ailing*, but to avoid the good old word *puke* we say *sick*. How much nobler to say: I *puked* all the way from Calais to Dover."

Lady Cunard had a horror of coarseness; but she made allowance for G. M.'s verbal eccentricities, which were more picturesque than the four-letter words in vogue today. And she was so sensitive to ridicule that she threw Sir Cecil Beaton's *Book of Beauty* into the fire lest the inclusion of her photograph expose her to the darts of enemies. For, of course, she had enemies even among those who accepted her invitations, since nowhere else in London, save possibly at the house of Lady Colefax, were they likely to hear such interesting conversation or meet celebrities whom the hostess inspired to sparkle.

Tired of Maud, her original name, Lady Cunard had exchanged it

LADY CUNARD

for Emerald, which gave her a feeling of rejuvenation. "Maud is too Tennysonian," she exclaimed, "it never suited me." The great difference between her receptions and those of other hostesses in London was the prevalence of music and literature; painting and politics were subsidiary. If senior politicians and financiers could be persuaded to support the arts she was prepared to cultivate them; but philistines and bores were excluded. Youth and beauty were necessary adjuncts, and she selected her beauty chorus with discrimination: these had much beside good looks to recommend them, for they kept her in touch with current events and contemporary movements. It was almost as if she had organized a repertory company of the *Commedia dell'Arte* whose members never knew in advance what roles had been allotted to them. The impromptu nature of the performance enhanced everybody's enjoyment. Those who proved inadequate were soon dismissed and forgotten.

"You are a hard woman in many ways, but if you were less hard I don't think you would have held me captive such a long time," George Moore wrote to her, and a hostess of her keen intelligence had to draw sharp lines; but her loyalty to old friends who had fallen on evil days was extreme: she went out of her way to help an exile from the Russian Revolution. She would pull every available string to procure a pension for a penurious poet and empty the contents of her purse. Her patronage of opera at a period when London society was lukewarm towards it was to absorb most of her fortune, as it had Sir Thomas Beecham's, derived from the much advertised liver pills. She was also an enlightened patron of ballet and the theatre, of the Old Vic and the Phoenix Society in particular, which offered such memorable performances of *The Duchess of Malfi* and other poetic dramas then seldom performed; and of the French *Compagnie des Quinze*. That beautiful play by Yeats, *The Hawk's Well*, had originally been performed in her drawing-room with masks and a setting by Dulac. In his *Conversations in Ebury Street* (1924), George Moore has paid her tribute:

> My admiration for this warmhearted, courageous woman compels me to praise her whenever her name is mentioned, and to recall to the remembrance of everybody that she is the one woman in London society whose thought for art extends beyond the narrow range of ordering a portrait to be painted and setting on foot an intrigue for the hanging of it in the National Gallery.

HAROLD ACTON

The rare and usually hilarious anachronisms at Emerald's dinners were due to her selfless devotion to opera and Sir Thomas Beecham: the two were indivisible. Potential supporters of Sir Thomas's Imperial League of Opera had to be cajoled, for in certain cases they were social climbers who hoped to meet Royalty at her house. Opera was the least of their concerns; they would chatter away through the most thrilling music. Emerald tolerated them for the sake of their financial contributions. To this day few, if any, opera houses are solvent without a state subsidy; and we then enjoyed nothing of the kind. An entire season depended on Emerald's strenuous efforts.

One of the funniest anachronisms that comes to mind was Mrs. Cory, a rich American who lived near Paris. As Mabelle Gilman she had played a leading role in the popular operatta *Floradora*, and captivated a steel-king, though some said he had been bewitched by her acrobatic diving at Palm Beach. Since then—who knows for what Freudian cause—she had grown discontented with the shape of her mouth and resorted to facial surgery with the result that her mouth, as if it had been sewn up at the corners, became so minute that she was asked to stop whistling in church. Her eyes looked immense by contrast, with an expression of perpetual amazement. And she had cause for amazement when George Moore sat next to her inveighing against chastity or motherhood or marriage. She had never heard such talk across the Atlantic. But when, taking her cue from G. M., she once uttered the word "brothel", Emerald pretended to be shocked and scolded her like a schoolgirl, I suspect for the fun of dramatizing a dull situation, since poor Mrs. Cory was dull apart from her eccentricities—I say "poor" because she was incredibly parsimonious. Guests at her French "sha-too" complained that she starved them. Disapproving of alcohol, she invariably turned her wine-glass upside down. Her favourite film was *Rio Rita*, which she had seen about twenty times. Her complete lack of humour was a foil to Emerald's wit; and when she sent a cheque for the League of Opera one felt it was a minor triumph. Unable to face her alone at Claridge's, Emerald would ask me to join them, and the conversation was pure Jabberwocky, though the meal was abstemious and frugal:

"You will have a lamb chop, *n'est-ce pas?* All Britishers love lamb chops, *le plat du pays.* I'll have some delicious mint sauce on my toast. And perhaps you care for ginger beer?"

LADY CUNARD

"No, Harold's used to wine. He comes from Italy."

Mrs. Cory took no notice: I had ginger beer. A Prime Minister's wife, whom Mrs. Cory had bribed with an evening gown to lunch with her the same day, seated at a neighbouring table, cut her dead.

"It is time you bought yourself a new dress, Mabelle," said Emerald. "You have a perfect Chanel figure."

"I am quite satisfied with Worth."

"He was all right for the Empress Eugénie when women wore bustles and crinolines, but you should modernize yourself. Sir Thomas tells me you have a lovely voice. I hope you will sing for us."

"I'm afraid of being too conspicuous."

"What nonsense!"

"Well, you must come with me to *Rio Rita*. I've bought the tickets. It's divine."

"I can't, as I'm going to *The Cherry Orchard*."

"Are cherries already in season? Do bring me some from your orchard. One can eat them and wear them in one's hat. . ."

Mrs. Corrigan, nicknamed Mrs. Cory-again, was another American benefactress of opera who seemed a big fish out of water at Emerald's gatherings. Perhaps because she had not been "accepted" by New York society, she was determined to compensate by making a splash with the *gratin* in Paris and the higher peerage in London. More lavishly opulent than Mrs. Cory and other competitors, and heedless of mockery, it was easy for her to succeed. Having rented the Hon. Mrs. George Keppel's house in Grosvenor Street, she dazzled the guests at her cotillions with golden souvenirs. But she, too, had scant sense of humour, and for all her jewels even Emerald could not make her sparkle. The imp in George Moore delighted in scandalizing her. I doubt if she had read one of his books; but she was a useful shock-absorber.

Emerald's vivacity was evidently due to her Irish-American ancestry. It flowed like champagne into the conversation and is impossible to recapture, whereas George Moore's voice may still be heard in his meandering rhythmic prose. Her enunciation was singularly sharp and clear, rising to shrillness in the heat of argument, and her choice of words betrayed her love of literature. Who else could pronounce "etiolate" with such effect? She revelled in the grandeur of Shakespearian English, and she could recite many unfamiliar passages by heart.

Other prominent Anglo-American social figures were Gladys, Duchess of Marlborough; Nancy, Lady Astor; and Sir Henry ("Chips") Channon. The Duchess, a classical beauty of subtle wit

HAROLD ACTON

and intellect, had been brought up in Europe under the cloud of a sensational domestic scandal; Lady Astor, a haughty Virginian, was the first woman to sit in the House of Commons; and Sir Henry Channon, another M. P., was a naturalized British subject from Chicago. These had little in common except a general antipathy. Proud of her aristocratic Virginian origin, Lady Astor tended to disparage her compatriots from the Far and Middle West as if they were related to Puccini's rollicking *Fanciulla*. Sir Harold Nicolson has recorded that she considered Lady Cunard and "Chips" Channon as "disintegrating influences" and deplored the fact that any but the best Virginian families should be received at Court. Sir Harold's own attitude, which reflected that of too many Englishmen of the period, was that "after all, every American is more or less as vulgar as any other American." (Half-American myself, I have never been able to fathom the depths of this parochial prejudice. There are shades of vulgarity even among the English; but they cannot be lumped together *en masse*.) With regard to Emerald, it must have been due to envy; for no other hostess in London could "hold a dinner-party audience entranced for an hour or more with her high spirits," as Sir Sacheverell Sitwell wrote. With her rival Lady Colefax, conversation rambled in a lower key; anything higher was liable to be interrupted, the celebrities seemingly hushed. Sir Harold felt more at home with Lady Colefax. He described Lady Cunard as "looking like a third-dynasty mummy painted pink by amateurs," and complained of a "ghastly dinner, supposed to be literary," where George Moore "talked rubbish about all great writers having lovely names. . . What a silly old man!" His fellow-guests on that occasion were "two Sitwells, Evelyn Waugh, and Robert Byron," who must have been hypnotized, as I was, by the veteran Irish novelist's chamber music.

However ghastly that evening had been, Nicolson could not resist returning to Emerald's; and he paid grudging tribute to her banderillero technique with Cabinet Ministers:

> Emerald is at her best. She well knows that Anthony Eden and Walter Elliot are not able to disclose what happened at the Cabinet this morning. Yet she also knows that by flagrant indiscretion she may get them to say something. 'Anthony,' she says, 'you are all wrong about Italy. Why should she not have Abyssinia? You must tell me that.'[2]

Personally, I most enjoyed her intimate parties, when Sir Thomas

Beecham would sit at the piano and play extracts from operas I had never heard by Méhul and Cjrétry and Handel, from whom he had selected the music for that enchanting ballet "The Gods Go a-Begging." His memory of sixteenth and seventeenth-century lyrics was remarkable; and he recited Edmund Waller's "Go, Lovely Rose," with a mellifluous unction I shall not forget. But such feasts were not for the worldlings.

Emerald slept so little that she spent half the night reading. Often she was impelled to discuss the novel or poem that engaged her with a friend, though this might waken him from slumber. The telephone would ring at two a.m. and, as if we were still at dinner, she would ask: "Tell me, Harold, have you ever heard a *castrato*? I believe they still exist in Rome, I suppose in the Papal choir. So many operas were composed for them in the eighteenth century that I would go to Rome to hear a male soprano."

"Surely there are plenty of eunuchs here in London, but I doubt if they have had musical training. Most of them are interior decorators. X. is certainly a eunuch and Y. giggles like one: perhaps he sings, he has a piercing voice. Why not give him an audution?"

"How wicked you are. I shall think of it when I meet them with Lady Colefax. I have been reading Balzac's story about Sarrasine, the cardinal's minion with whom a French artist fell in love. The young Frenchman believed him to be a woman, but I wonder. Could a male soprano pass as an attractive woman in real life?"

"In Balzac's time the subject was rather *risqué* and had to be treated with kid gloves. In these days a Thomas Mann could deal with it more frankly."

"You mean as in *Death in Venice*? What a haunting story. Thomas Mann is a great writer. Would you agree that his *Buddenbrooks* is far superior to *The Forsyte Sage*?"

And so she would discourse for half an hour or more, oblivious of time's wingéd chariot. It was usually some episode in Balzac or Richardson that excited her. Sometimes it was a character in Saint-Simon's memoirs who had suddenly roused her curiosity; and she wanted to know what had become of him or her in later life. After my return from China she would ask me questions about the Chinese theatre. She remembered her Chinese servants in San Francisco with special sympathy. Otherwise she never spoke of her youth: the records of her birth had conveniently been destroyed in the San Francisco earthquake of 1906. Nor did she speak of her marriage to the middle-aged Master of Hounds Sir Bache Cunard,

HAROLD ACTON

and of the fifteen years she had lived with him at Nevill Holt, the spacious manor near Market Harborough in Leicestershire, until, surfeited with country life, she parted from her husband and settled in London in 1911. Those years have been evoked tangentially by her daughter Nancy in her nostalgic *Memories of George Moore*.[3]

Alas, Nancy, who resembled her mother in so many ways and inherited her love of literature and music, must have borne her a deep grudge since childhood. This ill-feeling was under control when I first met her in 7 Grosvenor Square; and though she was aware of my affection for Her Ladyship, as she always called her, we became precarious friends. Apart from her feline, slightly macabre beauty, which had ravished Aldous Huxley and other contemporary writers, she had the passionate instincts of a genuine poet and a warmth of heart from which it seemed only her mother was excluded.

Few society hostesses (the word *salonnière* does not exist in French) are maternal or even conjugal by nature; it is likely that Emerald did not devote enough personal care to Nancy in childhood, though she provided her with what she considered the best education available. Amid the constant coming and going of house-guests at Holt, "smart and worldly, good riders to hounds and racegoers, men of wit and women of fashion, politicians and diplomats," little Nancy in her most impressionable years felt unduly neglected. She confessed that she felt—and was—entirely detached from both her parents, "admiring and critical of them by my own standards, those of a solitary child wondering much in silence how life was going to be."

Seeing Emerald and Nancy together, the physical resemblance between them was striking, almost uncanny; for there it ended—or did it? Emerald admired and tried to understand her, but Nancy was typical of the younger generation in revolt against Edwardian conventions. At the age of twenty she had married an unsuitable Australian officer against parental advice; and when the marriage broke up she resumed her maiden name. I thought of her as an ascetic voluptuary, for her liaisons were mainly cerebral—a pioneering evangelist of the *avant-garde* as her mother was an evangelist of the League of Opera. George Moore, whom she called her "first friend," had encouraged her to write and praised her first book of poems in the *Observer*. In Paris, where she settled on the Ile St. Louis, she became the exotic Muse of the Dadaists and surrealists, and founded a printing press of her own in the narrow

LADY CUNARD

rue Guénégaud, producing some twenty-four fantastically varied volumes, ranging from George Moore to Ezra Pound. Emerald approved of this enterprise, though she was worried by malicious reports of Nancy's Parisian avocations and experiments. Her enemies spread sinister rumours about her, culminating with that of a liaison with a black man, the genial pianist Henry Crowder. This led to their final rupture, when Nancy printed and circulated a cruelly vindictive pamphlet against her mother, best forgotten. Several friends attempted to reconcile them; but the virulence was all on Nancy's side. In her heart Emerald forgave her; and she often asked me for news of her in later years. "One can always forgive anyone who is ill," she said.

Nancy remained implacable. "I think of Her Ladyship, when at all, with great objectivity," she told Lady Diana Cooper. "She was at all times very far from me." "It's a matter of diamond cut diamond," was Norman Douglas's comment. But of the two diamonds Nancy's was the harder. Racial injustice monopolized her indignation until the outbreak of the Spanish civil war, when she espoused the republican cause with renewed fervour.

Entertaining day after day and helping to found the New Opera Syndicate with Sir Thomas Beecham; reading late at night when her guests had departed with music in their ears; Emerald had no time for introspection. Though she lived much in public, she armed her delicate frame against the invasion of publicity while continuing to fill her private stage with younger and more distinguished actors. The Prince of Wales had a leading role; so did the young Duke of Kent. Lady Diana Cooper was the reigning beauty; Phyllis de Janzé, Poppy Thursby, Lady Moore, Lady Bridget Parsons, were among the exquisite attendant graces. The "omnibus box" at Covent Garden was filled with the *jeunesse dorée*, who scarcely realized how subtly their taste was being educated. Indeed, Emerald often put me in mind of Steele's *Aspasia*: "to love her, is a liberal education".

While Sir Thomas Beecham was on the crest of the wave, surf-riding, as it were, above his orchestra and often singing in accompaniment to the score ("You were in fine voice, Sir Thomas." "Well, *somebody* had to sing the opera!") George Moore was suffering from the infirmities of old age. He lamented his impotency more than his uremia, whose symptoms and treatment he would describe in lurid detail to bewildered dowagers at luncheon with Emerald. Though he was an acknowledged master of English prose narrative nearing eighty, he had never received official recognition, whereas lesser luminaries were honoured with knighthoods and university degrees. Appealing to Lord Balfour and Arnold Bennett to exert themselves in his behalf, Emerald tried in vain to secure him the Order of Merit. All she could achieve was to persuade the Prince of Wales to give him a private audience. The veteran novelist was immensely elated by this gracious gesture, which more than compensated for his neglect by officialdom. "Oh! I can't tell you what I think of the Prince. The great work he is doing. . ."

Emerald took him for drives in Richmond Park, "and when I am with you," he wrote, "the thought entertains me all the while, that I am the luckiest man in the world." He died peacefully on January 21, 1933; and all his pictures and furniture, with a few exceptions, were bequeathed to Lady Cunard. The pictures adorned her walls; but with characteristic generosity she distributed many of his objects among old friends. Eventually some 276 letters—a fraction of those he had sent her during forty years—were left to Sir Sacheverell Sitwell, who entrusted them to Sir Rupert Hart-Davis for publication (1957). Through these letters we see how deeply he was devoted to Emerald, long after passion was spent. "You are all I have," he wrote. "It is through you that I know that I am alive." And again: "I think of you as I have always done, as a joy that knows no diminishing—you are the magic apple which however much one eats of it never grows less." Her "genius to make a work of art out of life itself" was the recurrent motif of his musings; and those who appreciated her qualities would agree that his eulogy was not exaggerated.

Because of her long-standing friendship with the Prince of Wales, who enjoyed her company and the carefree atmosphere she created, it was natural that Emerald should entertain the elegant American from Baltimore who had conquered his affections; and again her enemies invented preposterous stories about her aims and ambitions at an Anglo-American court in the event of the Prince's marriage; but Emerald was by no means the only hostess to cultivate Mrs. Simpson. Ladies Colefax and Oxford were equal competitors for her attention; but Emerald, as a Californian, was singled out for censure, notably by the Virginian Lady Astor, who wanted to lecture the new King on the deplorable effect of this equivocal relationship in Canada and the United States. Emerald was blamed as if she were the go-between. Undoubtedly Edward VIII's abdication proved a bitter disappointment; but her distress was only communicated to "Chips" Channon.

Emerald happened to be in New York with Sir Thomas Beecham when war was declared in 1939. Despite her attachment to the eminent conductor and her hatred of war, absence from her dearest friends in London became all the more painful when she discovered by chance that Sir Thomas, then on a concert tour in Canada, was engaged to marry the pianist Betty Humby. After almost thirty years of complete dedication, the news, tactlessly blurted out at a formal luncheon, was like a dagger thrust. Sir Thomas had been a cold man, she reflected. Perhaps his very coldness, as in the case of Horace Walpole and Madame du Deffand, had held her in captivity. To quote Lytton Strachey on that subject, "If he had cared for her a little more, perhaps she would have cared for him a good deal less."

But it was her worship of his musical genius and the fact that they did not live together that bound her to Sir Thomas. By hook or by crook she was determined to return to England, a voyage fraught with danger and discomfort, since she would have to fly from Lisbon and the high altitude racked her ears. But Emerald was fearless.

Her house had been hit by a bomb and would have been impossible to maintain in wartime; but, as Madame du Deffand had established herself in a smart convent, Emerald found rooms on the seventh floor of the Dorchester Hotel. These she furnished in her own style, that of eighteenth-century France, by adapting her console-tables, cabinets and commodes to their reduced scale. The fragrance of her personality became concentrated in this smaller space. Most of her diminished income was spent on entertainment. Her parties were as varied as before and as cosmopolitan, though never more than eight sat down to a dinner as palatable as could be provided amid the prevailing restrictions. When French wines were scarce, Tony Gandarillas supplied vintages from Chile. On my return from India, Emerald was the first person I visited; and I marvelled at her indomitable spirit.

The war was all around us, bursting and crashing above and below; yet it failed to penetrate that seventh floor apartment or pollute the conversation. There were deafening moments to which Emerald paid no attention. "War is so vulgar," she remarked. No air-raid shelters for her! The raids had the negative advantage of detaining her guests, prolonging a discussion of Proust until ululation of the "All Clear".

HAROLD ACTON

Duff Cooper (Viscount Norwich) has recorded in his autobiography that in June 1944, before returning to Algiers at General de Gaulle's request, he dined at the Dorchester with Emerald.

> It was the night of the first attack by unpiloted planes. My hostess, who disliked the war, but knew no fear and lived on the seventh floor of the hotel, was most indignant when she was informed of what was happening, declared it was quite impossible and only showed how stupid people became in wartime that they could believe such rubbish. One of the hotel servants, on the other hand, said it was very good sign, as it proved how short of men the Germans were, that they were obliged to send their aeroplanes over empty.

From tea-time onwards she would receive a floating company of visitors, many of them in uniform; and some brought books and embroidered their gossip with fantasies, amusing enough on the spur of the moment; but, as George Moore remarked in one of his letters to her, gossip "loses its character when it is written down: ink is an adjuvant which develops a dangerous quality in harmless ingredients." To drop the names of her numerous visitors would be tedious. Cyril Connolly, Peter Quennell and John Lehmann stimulated her interest in recent publications; and Nancy Mitford brought literary refreshment from the bookshop where she was working. When she liked a budding author, she gave dozens of his books to the influential in politics or diplomacy who listened to her advice.

Her movements and gestures were still those of a much younger woman: her little feet stepped out of a scene of *Dalliance* by Fragonard. Enemies as well as friends had always compared her to a bird; and the analogy, so often repeated, is inescapable, for it was obvious. George Moore had written:"I can think of nothing more like her than a bird, for she has the bright eyes of a bird, and she in instinctive and courageous as a sparrow-hawk." Her powerful rival, Mrs. Ronnie Greville, had compared her to a yellow canary and nicknamed her "the Lollipop". Her appetite also was that of a sparrow; she hardly ate enough to nourish herself. While others guzzled, she sipped. One wondered what fed the flame of her exuberance.

The postwar world of self-righteous austerity was definitely not her oyster. But she still had congenial escorts to concerts and Covent Garden, her chief spiritual resource if not her religion. So

LADY CUNARD

gallantly did she conceal it with laughter and persiflage that few realized the secret sadness of her predicament. At a gala ball—or was it a grand wedding reception?—soon after the war, her ebullient friend "Chips" Channon remarked with gusto: "*This* is what we have been fighting for!" Emerald retorted ironically: "Oh why, dear? Do you mean they are all Poles?" Remembering Prince André Poniatowski and other Polish friends, our unilateral guarantee to Poland and its aftermath still rankled. Serenity was not one of her attributes. For nearly thirty years all her social activities had revolved round Sir Thomas Beecham; and now the ultra-violet rays of his dynamism no longer reached her. She was as cut off from him as from her daughter Nancy.

Her rooms at the Dorchester seemed to have shrunk like her existence. The Impressionist paintings by Monet and Guillaumin above her sofa reminded her that she must look through G. M.'s letters. Those which were too embarrassing must be destroyed. His admirers insisted that they should be published sooner or later. She had refused to show them to Charles Morgan, who felt he could not write his biography without them. What was she to do? G. M. had been the most assiduous of her correspondents, partly because he would never install a telephone in his house; and a telephone was indispensable to Emerald. The question remained in suspense.

It was in San Francisco, her birthplace, that I heard of Emerald's death on July 10, 1948; and I thought of how different her life would have been had she remained there, and what a loss to music in England, and to the joy and wit and colour of London society. That society had ceased to exist: there are no longer hostesses of her calibre.

She who never thought of illness had latterly been more ill than she suspected. Pneumonia, pleurisy, and an incurable malady of the throat combined to kill her. Her last words were to offer champagne to her devoted Scotch maid Mary Gordon and her attendant nurse. She could sip only a spoonful herself. Her ashes were scattered in Grosvenor Square, a corner of which had been beautified by her radiant personality.

NOTES

1. *Conversations in Ebury Street*, p. 26.
2. *Diaries and Letters*, 1930-1939 (London, 1966), p. 211.
3. London, 1956.

HAROLD ACTON

Composed in Souvenir by
New Republic Books,
Washington, D.C.

Printed and bound by
The Maple Press
York, Pennsylvania

Book design by
Lynette Ruschak

Typesetting by
Marlene Davis
Peggy Magee
Sylvia Bowden
Deborah Wilson
Nancy Stockwell

Paste-up by
Kenneth Grady
Jill Hofmann
Lydia Inglett